More INFANT *and* TODDLER *Experiences*

**FRAN HAST
ANN HOLLYFIELD**

Redleaf Press®
www.redleafpress.org
800-423-8309

Published by Redleaf Press
10 Yorkton Court
St. Paul, MN 55117
www.redleafpress.org

Cover design by Jim Handrigan
Cover photo © Sergey Makarenko/Veer
Printed in the United States of America

Library of Congress Cataloging-in-Publication Data
Hast, Fran.
  More infant and toddler experiences / Fran Hast and Ann Hollyfield.
    p. cm.
  Includes index.
  ISBN 978-1-929610-14-3 (paper)
  1. Day care centers—United States. 2. Infants—Care—United States. 3. Toddlers—Care—United States. 4. Early childhood education—United States. 5. Child development—United States. I. Hollyfield, Ann. II. Title.
HQ778.63 .H383 2001
362.71'2—dc21
                                                                                    2001044101

Printed on acid-free paper

Acknowledgments

We are indebted to those past caregivers at the Palo Alto Infant-Toddler Center (ITC) who embraced the vision and were able to build the foundation with us before moving on: Cheryl, Clare, Johanna, Kate E., Kathy, Lasana, Maggie, Marianne, Maryann, Nancy, Ro, Ruth, Ted, and many others who carry part of ITC wherever they go. We are grateful to them for their modeling, support, and assistance.

A special note of thanks to our current coworkers at ITC who put up with flexible schedules and continue to share their creativity: Amy, Brenda, Jill, Katya, Mojgan, Nena, Terry, and Vanessa.

We also appreciate the assistance of Carol, Patricia, Marydawn, Elizabeth, and the children at Neighborhood Infant/Toddler Center.

We are indebted to Palo Alto Community Child Care, which continues to champion our book writing. The administrative staff—Cara, Janice, Judy, Lanie, Lisa, Lori, Margo, and Peter—encourage us in ways that expand our professionalism.

We are grateful to Janet Gonzalez-Mena, who has personally and professionally acknowledged our work. She continues to model the importance of personal growth and multicultural perspectives to caregiving.

Most recently, studies about how young children learn have galvanized us to share our teaching experience with more people. In particular, we thank Alison Gopnik and her coauthors for making such research readable and accessible in the book *The Scientist in the Crib: Minds, Brains, and How Children Learn* (New York: Morrow, 1999).

ITC families, past and present, provide invaluable support for our extracurricular work by providing an essential sense of community from which to write. Our own families continue to model an interest in the world and support for one another.

Thanks to all at Redleaf Press, who gave us another opportunity, especially our editor, Beth. With much laughter and patience, she maintains a perspective about what is important and really understands our passions for infant/toddler caregiving.

*To those caregivers who choose to enrich their lives
and communities with their commitment to children
rather than enriching themselves materially.*

*To those caregivers who made the painful choice
to leave the early childhood field; we hope you will consider
a return to the profession that needs you.*

And to Mark, Chief Cook and CFO.

Contents

Introduction   1

Chapter 1
Reviewing the Foundation   5

Chapter 2
Planning Environments to Support Infants' and Toddlers' Learning   13

Chapter 3
Planned Experiences for Infants and Toddlers   35

Index   175

Introduction

Since the publication of *Infant and Toddler Experiences* in 1999, we have been gratified by the response from parents, students, and other caregivers who work "on the floor" with infants and toddlers and found our book helpful. We hope that this new book will also contribute to the field by giving caregivers confidence in their ability to do their job well, increasing their enjoyment of the children they care for, and supporting increased quality care for children under three.

Sadly, child care is in a deeper crisis than it was two years ago. There is a serious shortage of experienced caregivers throughout the country. Caregiver wages are extremely low in relation to other skilled professions. Few people are attracted to the field. Committed caregivers who stay on the job feel compromised in doing the job they want to do for children. When they have to spend time on the job training inexperienced caregivers or extend their hours to cover staff shortages, many of them burn out and leave the field. Thus, an already high rate of turnover puts stress on those who remain in the field, and turnover is perpetuated.

Quality child care for infants and toddlers depends upon nurturing, long-term connections with their caregivers, other children, and their families. The high rate of caregiver turnover leads to inconsistent care for many infants and toddlers. When long-term connections are impossible to achieve, children's optimum development is jeopardized. Inexperienced caregivers often lack the knowledge to respond appropriately to children and their families. The vicious circle of caregivers leaving the field, unhappy children and families, and inexperienced caregivers means that few people involved with child care have a quality experience.

Ironically, at the same time, a growing body of research confirms the importance of early child care and education. In *The Scientist in the Crib: Minds, Brains, and How Children Learn* (New York: Morrow, 1999), Alison Gopnik, Andrew N. Meltzoff, and Patricia K. Kuhl affirm what attentive caregivers have long known: the predisposition of children is to learn and that of adults is to be available to guide them.

This research also confirms the importance of day-to-day experiences of humans in their first three years of life and points out that, just as public schools were developed for older children, there is a need to acknowledge that "being in the company of caring adults is school for babies" (Gopnik 1999, 205). Care and teaching are inseparable; the same actions that nurture babies give them the kinds of information they need as they experiment to find out how objects move in space, what other minds are thinking, and how to decipher language. Human brains are designed to work within a social network. Everyday experiences with caring adults in the crib, kitchen, and backyard provide evidence that lets an infant revise her initial theories and extend her experimentation. This is why artificial interventions to speed up development, such as flash cards for babies, are at best useless and at worst distractions from the babies' natural drive to learn through interactions. The strategies we propose are intended to support these daily interactions, not supplant them. In this book, as in *Infant and Toddler Experiences,* we offer a way for teachers to think about what they do with infants and toddlers in light of what we know about early development, in the hopes of reforming caregiving practices.

Infant/toddler caregiving requires special knowledge and training. Programs for infants and toddlers must be based on infant/toddler development rather than reflect a watered-down version of preschool practices. There are few accessible, practical resources that lend themselves to on-the-job training for beleaguered infant/toddler caregivers. We want this book to be an additional resource for infant/toddler caregivers to use as they "grow themselves" in the field.

Other professionals, such as the staff at the Center for the Childcare Workforce in Washington, D.C., are working diligently to solve the problem of inadequate compensation for caregivers. Our contribution is to offer ideas for ways of interacting with infants and toddlers that can increase caregivers' enjoyment of the children in their care. Underpaid caregivers may stay in the field when they find their jobs rewarding. When caregivers have the tools to meet the challenge of this difficult job, their satisfaction comes from their increasing skills and the difference they can make to young children and their families. Caregiver satisfaction can help reduce the turnover that is rampant in our field.

When a program works well for children, caregivers are more likely to feel competent and enjoy their work. In *Infant and Toddler Experiences,* we suggest strategies for interacting with young children that support the developing child as well as the caregiver learning on the job. In this book, *More Infant and Toddler Experiences,* we describe an environment that supports caregivers using these strategies. When children's behaviors are seen as problems, caregivers can often find the solutions in altering the environment to meet the developmental needs of all the infants and toddlers in the group.

As we finish this book, Ann marvels that twenty years in the field have passed. The day-to-day joy of caring for young children is central to her commitment of "spreading the word" through workshops and writing books. Fran has spent half of her life (so far!) working with infants, toddlers, their families, and other caregivers. She is continually renewed by the long-term connections and invigorated by new research about the brain and learning. We continue to do workshops and write books because we strongly believe in the value of our philosophy to our communities. We believe it can help caregivers make the difference they want to make in the lives of young children and their families. We receive knowledge and practical ideas from others that inspires us to stay and learn in the field, and we want to pass it on by sharing our experience. We urge caregivers who are new to the field to stick with it, stretching your knowledge and understanding while making connections with others in your child care community.

We can be proud to take part honorably in this most human endeavor and to recognize as worthy the pursuit we have chosen. This is, in fact, why we are writing this book. We want to share a spark of passion with the reader: the joy of seeing infants and toddlers learn from the everyday experiences in their lives.

Fran Hast and Ann Hollyfield
April 2001

Contact Information

We appreciate your feedback on the usefulness of this book and *Infant and Toddler Experiences*.

Please e-mail us: itexperience@aol.com

Or write to us:
Palo Alto Infant-Toddler Center
4111 Alma Street
Palo Alto, CA 94306

Reviewing the Foundation

I n *Infant and Toddler Experiences,* we discuss ten principles that guide our interactions with infants and toddlers and seven strategies that we use to apply the principles to our everyday work with children. We will briefly review the principles and strategies in this chapter. If you are not familiar with them, it's a good idea to refer to the first volume, *Infant and Toddler Experiences,* for more detail.

Definitions

Infants: Children from birth to approximately twelve months who may be mobile but are not yet walking.

Toddlers: Children who are walking, up to three years of age.

Caregiver: An adult who is caring for a child. This includes parents or anyone who lives with or is responsible for a child.

The Ten Principles

The following "Ten Principles of Respectful Care," adapted from the work of Janet Gonzalez-Mena and Dianne Widmeyer Eyer, guide our interactions with young children.

The Ten Principles of Respectful Caregiving

1. Involve infants and toddlers in things that concern them. Don't work around them or distract them to get the job done faster.

2. Invest in quality time. Don't settle for supervising groups, without focusing (more than just briefly) on individual children.

3. Learn each child's unique ways of communicating (cries, words, movements, gestures, facial expressions, body positions) and teach them yours. Don't underestimate children's ability to communicate even though their verbal language skills may be nonexistent or minimal.

4. Invest time and energy to build a total person (concentrate on the "whole child"). Don't focus on cognitive development alone or look at it as separate from total development.

5. Respect infants and toddlers as worthy people. Don't treat them as objects or cute little empty-headed people to be manipulated.

6. Be honest about your feelings around infants and toddlers. Don't pretend to feel something that you don't or pretend not to feel something that you do.

7. Model the behavior you want to teach. Don't preach.

8. Recognize problems as learning opportunities, and let infants and toddlers try to solve their own. Don't rescue them, constantly make life easy for them, or try to protect them from all problems.

9. Build security by teaching trust. Don't teach distrust by being undependable or often inconsistent.

10. Be concerned about the *quality* of development in each stage. Don't rush infants and toddlers to meet developmental milestones.

Here's a scene illustrating some of these principles in an infant/toddler child care setting.

Ten-month-old Erin pulls up on a wooden railing. She picks up a three-inch ball, drops it, then picks up a clear yellow bowl and looks through it at the caregiver, Lee. As in a peekaboo game, Erin pulls the bowl away from her face, grinning, and repeats this action seven times. Erin squats down to sit on her knees. Rocking back, she tips and falls in slow motion, banging her arm against the wood railing. Erin lies there quietly for five seconds. Lee responds, "Oh, you tipped over. Can you get up by yourself?" Erin throws her legs to one side to right herself, then returns to the peekaboo game, repeating it three more times before crawling off to pick up a rubber toy.

Meanwhile, two-year-old Roni is lying in the beanbag chair with her doll and its blanket. Previously she had been changing its diaper and putting it to sleep. Talking to the doll quietly in Hebrew, Roni twirls her own hair to remove a clip. She hands it to Lee. "I can tell you are tired and ready for a nap," Lee acknowledges. "It will be story time soon, then nap time. You can wait on the pillow or in the rocking chair." Roni settles on the pillow with her doll.

Thirteen-month-old Avi is just arriving with his mom. He spies Erin and points and smiles as he leans out of his mother's arm. Lee comments, "I see you're happy to see Erin, Avi. After you say hi and play a bit, I have your lunch ready when you want to eat." Avi's mom, Sue, sits on the floor with him and begins to share information about Avi's morning with Lee. Three minutes later, Avi crawls to the cube chairs, kneels next to one, pulling up with his upper body, and looks at Lee. "Oh, I can tell you're ready to eat! Let's pull the chair out to sit and wash up," she says to him.

Notice how the caregiver applies specific principles in familiar everyday experiences. Lee did not rescue Erin when she toppled over, as sug-

See pages 11–19 of *Infant and Toddler Experiences* for a full discussion of each principle and related scenarios.

The Seven Comprehensive Strategies

An infant/toddler caregiver's job is to lend support, acknowledge children's effort, and facilitate each child's development. The seven strategies that follow will help caregivers apply the ten principles in daily routine and play situations. Using them helps caregivers to support children's development.

The routines of transition, sleeping, eating, and diapering take up a large part of the caregiving day in an infant/toddler center. From the child's point of view, these are all equally valuable experiences: play is not better than diapering, eating is not better than singing. Each experience offers opportunity for interaction and learning. The strategies help caregivers use every opportunity throughout a child's day to support their development and nurture relationships.

Using the strategies also makes the day's routines go more smoothly for the caregiver. For

gested by Principle #8 (recognize problems as learning opportunities). Lee responded calmly and offered Erin a way to solve her own predicament. Principles #3 (communication) and #5 (respect) are evident as Lee responds to Roni's cues for a nap when she twirls her hair and removes her hair clip. Lee's response acknowledges Roni's ability to know when she is tired and ready to sleep. Lee has learned Roni's ways of communicating and is mindful to respond and model communication with all the babies from the beginning. Finally, look at Lee's interaction with Avi as she dependably has his lunch ready to serve after his arrival, reflecting Principle #9 (build security by being dependable).

example, a caregiver can involve children in routines that affect them when they anticipate transitions. When a caregiver shares information—"In two minutes it will be time for lunch"—a child is drawn in to the process of a transition. This gives the toddler time to finish what he is doing and plan to move on. Infants and toddlers both respond by being less resistant. When the time has come to move or transition, the child is more likely to participate because he is involved. The caregiver experiences a more pleasant time with the child as they join together to accomplish routine tasks. Making repeated cooperative connections of this kind builds rewarding relationships. For a full discussion of the use of strategies during routines, see *Infant and Toddler Experiences*, pages 50–55, 121–125, and 194–200.

The Seven Comprehensive Strategies

1. Observe individual children; provide for optimal stress.

2. Model the behavior you wish to see.

3. Acknowledge children's feelings.

4. Anticipate transitions, unusual events, and changes in routines.

5. Help children articulate their needs and wants.

6. Offer real choices.

7. Set consistent limits.

1. Observe individual children; provide for optimal stress

By paying attention to individual children as they make their way through the environment, caregivers learn their interests, needs, and range of skills.

When a caregiver knows a child's abilities and interests, she can offer the child opportunities to practice current skills as well as to take the next developmental step. Janet Gonzalez-Mena describes this as "optimal stress": just enough of a challenge to be interesting to the child, but not one so overwhelming as to be defeating or overly frustrating. Guided by their observations, caregivers can provide optimal stress by setting up the environment to be appealing and challenging rather than frustrating for the individuals in the group. For example, a caregiver can place a favorite toy barely within an infant's reach or provide a ramp as a challenging option for children pushing or riding wheeled toys.

2. Model the behavior you wish to see

The importance of modeling behavior cannot be overestimated. Children observe what goes on around them as a keen learning tool. Young children naturally desire to do what adults do in order to participate in the world around them and figure out how it works. For this reason, caregivers will see their attitudes and actions reflected by the children, and it is not respectful to expect behavior from children that adults do not practice themselves. For example, caregivers should always sit when eating if that is expected of the children. Or, since grabbing toys away is not okay, a caregiver would model for a child who tries to grab a toy from the caregiver by saying, "I'm using this right now. Your turn next." Five seconds later, the caregiver can follow through: "I'm finished! Now it's your turn—thanks for waiting." When an adult allows a child to grab a toy from her, the child will learn it is okay to grab toys from anyone, including other children.

3. Acknowledge children's feelings

What is more comforting than the assurance that your feelings are okay, that how you feel is accepted? There is lifelong value for infants and toddlers in learning to accept and express a wide range of feelings in order to practice appropriate responses to everyday situations. Caregivers can help young children express their feelings without hurting themselves or others. For example, "I can tell you're frustrated, but I can't let you hit Tran; you can use your arm to throw the soft ball or hit the pillow," "Did you want to say hi? You can use your arm to wave hi to Renato," or

"I can see you playing with the hoops together; isn't that fun?"

4. Anticipate transitions, unusual events, and changes in routines

Most people like to know what is going to happen next. Children are no exception. Therefore, the caregiving day goes much more easily when caregivers tell them what to expect. Often children are told to stop what they are doing because the caregiver knows it's time to do something else. As a result, children usually resist what is being demanded of them because they are so focused in the moment. To show respect for what a child is doing, caregivers can say ahead of time what's going to happen. This strategy gives a child time to process the information and join in the next experience, and it is a simple sharing of information, not a warning: "Remember, Amber, your dad's picking you up early today so you can go see the doctor."

5. Help children articulate their needs and wants

This strategy supports young children as they practice language and learn to connect it with their needs and personal preferences. Even tiny babies express preferences by turning their head toward or away from a presented object. Caregivers can reflect this by saying out loud, "I see you really like the banana in your cereal." To support toddlers' growing autonomy, caregivers can give them the words to express their needs and wants. For example, a child may say "mo" when he wants more of something. The caregiver can respond, "More juice, you want more juice." Or if a child often uses the word "mine," the caregiver can acknowledge feelings first ("I can tell you want to play with the truck"), then give him words to use with other children ("Tell

Yukiko, 'my turn next'"). We do not advocate telling children to share; we feel it is not developmentally appropriate, nor respectful. There is a full discussion of this topic in *Infant and Toddler Experiences*, pages 128–129.

6. Offer real choices

One of the great lessons of life is that we always have a choice. Just as tiny babies can express preferences, older infants and toddlers can learn to make choices. Caregivers can acknowledge that a child has preferences and honor those preferences by offering real choices. Infants and toddlers benefit from making choices because it involves them in the processes of their lives and provides practice for decision making. At snack time, a caregiver may offer a choice: "Would you like a blue cup or a green cup?" Ryan says, "I want a purple cup." "Oh, I'm sorry, there are blue and green cups on the tray today; no purple cups. Which would you like?" the caregiver explains. The other piece of the lesson is that in life, we don't always get to choose the alternatives.

7. Set consistent limits

Setting limits consistently provides infants and toddlers with reliable results to their testing behaviors. If limits change from hour to hour or day to day, it is confusing for young children intent on figuring out the world. Since they draw conclusions about how the world works by testing their ideas, inconsistent limits force them to test and retest. (And it's a waste of their time, too!) Consistent limits allow a child to learn what behaviors are okay. A consistent response

and follow-through allows infants and toddlers to use their energy for exploring the environment with fewer interruptions.

In setting limits, we use a guideline we learned years ago from Janet Gonzalez-Mena, "For every no give two yeses." When we use this guideline, we clearly state the limit: "I can't let you throw the dish," and immediately give the toddler a choice of two ways to fulfill his goal: "You can throw the ball or this balled-up sock." Repeated experience with caregivers who use this guideline provides toddlers opportunities to accumulate information that helps them to make more appropriate choices. (For more detail regarding the Seven Comprehensive Strategies, see *Infant and Toddler Experiences*, pages 28–41.)

Let's revisit Lee in the infant room with the two infants, Erin and Avi, and toddler Roni. We will point out how Lee uses these strategies to support each child's development.

Remember when Erin toppled over and Lee's response was not to jump up and rescue her? Lee uses the strategy of *observation and optimal stress* when she calmly offers Erin the opportunity to solve her own predicament: "Can you get up by yourself?"

Lee applies two other strategies—*acknowledging feelings* and *offering real choices*—in response to Roni's nonverbal communication of twirling her hair and removing her hair clip: "I can tell you are tired and ready for a nap. It will be story time then nap time very soon. You can wait on the pillow or in the rocking chair." Lee names Roni's feelings for her ("I can tell you are tired . . .") and then offers her a choice of appropriate ways to tend to her own weariness.

And finally, Lee uses the strategy of *anticipation* after Avi's arrival. She builds his security and trust by *anticipating* his transition to lunch: "After you say hi and play a bit, I have your lunch ready when you want to eat." Lee also helps Avi learn to *articulate his needs and wants* by responding to his nonverbal language when he crawls to the table and cube chair: "Oh, I can see you're ready to eat! Let's pull out the chair to sit and wash up."

Caregivers have told us that using the strategies helps them focus on and really be with the children. When caregivers use them, their interactions with children become reciprocal, much like a conversation.

These strategies are not magic. Your caregiving day will not be instantly transformed into a walk along a sandy trail by the sea of tranquility. But as you learn to use the strategies, you will be able to anticipate the rising tide in order to avoid being swamped by children's demands.

Planning Environments to Support Infants' and Toddlers' Learning

In chapter 1 we reviewed the principles and strategies we find helpful in supporting caring interactions between infants, toddlers, and their caregivers. Sometimes, however well-intentioned a caregiver may be, on-the-job frustrations make it difficult to carry out and sustain these interactions. In this chapter we will explore ideas for planning environments that support infant/toddler learning and enable quality interactions, thus making the caregiver's work more enjoyable.

It has been our observation that caregiver frustrations can be related to children's frustrations. Children's frustrations are often linked to the physical environment in ways that are not immediately obvious. If the environment does not work for children, they become frustrated when their needs for free exploration, close relationships, and skill practice are not met. Their behavior is in turn frustrating for caregivers. When the environment works for children, the caregiver's job is much easier. Everyone moves more smoothly through the environment with fewer disruptions. This allows more opportunity for caregivers to have nurturing interactions with infants and toddlers. In order to understand children's frustrations, it's important for caregivers to think about how the physical environment can be a barrier to meeting infant/toddler developmental needs.

Understanding Infants' and Toddlers' Everyday Behaviors

In order to understand how the physical environment can influence their efforts to meet children's developmental needs, caregivers first have to know and understand infant/toddler development. It is helpful to have an understanding of the general sequence and important milestones of children's development as a context in which to place the behaviors caregivers see every day.

Communication

(relates to language development)

Honor both nonverbal and verbal communication, and respond with respect to child-initiated interactions.

The attitude we communicate determines the quality of each interaction.

Curiosity
(relates to cognitive development)

Child Tasks

Use senses to explore environment to construct own reality

Discover cause and effect

Assimilate knowledge

Caregiver Strategies

Provide choices of materials and time to manipulate them.

Validate the child's experience ("say what you see").

Plan to extend the exploration using the child's interests as a guide.

Offer information ("say what you know").

Promote self-awareness.

Share the caregiver's interests ("say who you are").

Connection
(relates to social-emotional development)

Child Tasks

Develop self-concept
Trust

Autonomy

Build relationships with peers, family, caregivers

Learn to resolve conflict
Take responsibility and experience the consequences of actions
With self
With others

Caregiver Strategies

Be predictable and consistent in meeting children's needs.

Slow the pace; be an "island."

Introduce peers and adults by name.

Include family culture.

Affirm mutual interests to encourage interdependence.

Be aware of one's own internal conflict.

Help children learn to resolve conflicts.

Coordination
(relates to physical development and integration of skills)

Child Tasks

Negotiate relationship with gravity and space
Balance
Mobility
Control
Strength
Large/Small motor

Integration of skills

Problem solving

Caregiver Strategies

Provide opportunities for practice at varied levels of skill.

Promote body awareness by coaching.

Make room for trial and error and repeated investigation.

Allow for innovative use of materials.

Facilitate problem solving with observation and open-ended questions.

Comprehensive Strategies That Support Caring Interactions

- Observe individual children; provide for Optimal Stress
- Model the behavior you wish to see
- Acknowledge Children's Feelings
- Anticipate transitions, unusual events, and changes in routine
- Help Children Articulate their Needs and Wants
- Offer Real Choices
- Set Consistent Limits

This chart summarizes the behavior caregivers see expressed by young children in routine and play experiences and presents coinciding approaches for caring interactions. Please note that development of the whole child is a continuing and overlapping process.

Attentive caregivers can identify children's stages of development by the behaviors they exhibit. Caregivers can think of these behaviors as evidence of the developmental tasks they are practicing. Children are actually telling us what developmental steps they are taking. For example, we know an infant who puts objects in her mouth is exploring her environment in a way that's appropriate for her development. Similarly, a toddler who won't let you put on her socks because she wants to do it herself is expressing her drive for autonomy. We find it helpful to

think about infant and toddler developmental tasks by dividing the behaviors caregivers witness into three broad categories: curiosity, connections, and coordination. See the chart on the opposite page for a list of children's developmental tasks associated with the three C's, and ways that caregivers can support those tasks.

Curiosity: Curiosity is what drives children's *cognitive development*—the expression of a child's natural drive to understand through exploration. We see evidence of curiosity when an infant turns toward a sound or "tastes" an interesting texture with her tongue. A toddler will pour, pound, drop, and mix objects to see how they react. Infants and toddlers rely on their senses to construct their own reality by investigating their environment.

Connection: Connection is the key to children's *social and emotional development*. Infants and toddlers need a strong foundation of trust and autonomy. When infants' needs are met consistently, they learn to trust that they will be cared for in a friendly world. This security enables the toddler to experience risky venturing away from familiar situations. As social beings, infants and toddlers connect with their caregivers, their peers, themselves, and their environment to forge interdependent relationships. As described by Alison Gopnik and her coauthors in *The Scientist in the Crib: Minds, Brains, and How Children Learn* (New York: Morrow, 1999), young children are programmed to direct their own learning within an emotional context; they know how to use others to learn.

Coordination: Coordination is at the center of young children's *physical development*. As young children develop physically, caregivers know they will roll, creep, sit up, crawl, walk, run, jump, and climb. With opportunities to negotiate gravity and space, they fall down, pick themselves up, crawl through, and practice acting on objects. Infants and toddlers play with balance, mobility, strength, and control as they integrate their skills through continual problem solving: How can I reach the rattle? Where does my body fit? What marks can I make with this

paint brush? Young children use their bodies to answer many questions like these.

Current research tells us that infants and toddlers think more and differently than even doting grandmothers imagined. As Alison Gopnik points out, researchers have learned through carefully crafted observations that human babies are born knowing how to organize the information from their senses. They know a great deal about their links with other people, understand that they live in a three-dimensional world, and can categorize the sounds of language they hear. They are also endowed with abilities that make learning itself innate and are programmed to experiment in order to learn more. At the same time, adult humans are programmed to nurture this development. Of special relevance to infant/toddler caregivers is the rapid change in thinking and perception that takes place from the emotional connections between a child and an adult during the first three years of life.

Play is what children's learning looks like to adults. Infants and toddlers observe how the world works and experiment to confirm their ideas. As they observe the results, they retest until they are sure of the outcome. For example, infants and toddlers "practice gravity" by repeatedly dropping objects and watching them fall. Infants will practice dropping their food or spoons to the floor, looking expectantly at the floor as the object falls. It's easy for adults to get exasperated with this behavior when they forget that children need to be sure the object will always fall. Two-and-a-half-year-old Ben throws a sheet of paper up into the air, saying, "I'm throwing the paper; I want it to break." Ben is obviously testing what he's been told: "Things will break if you throw them." Children at all levels of development use what looks like play to build experience to confirm their ideas. Planning environments that allow this natural investigation is crucial to infant and toddler development.

What do we mean by an environment? An environment is any area in which infants and toddlers have the freedom to move and play. An infant/toddler program may have several environments. An enclosed room would be one environment. An outside yard would be another environment. We suggest caregivers look at each room or area as a separate environment.

What Happens When Environments Don't Take Development into Account

In many centers, environmental planning for infants and toddlers lacks a developmental foundation. Planning may be limited to teacher-directed "activities" or based on themes that spring from teachers' interests rather than from the children's natural passions. Caregivers may put out a haphazard arrangement of toys, either too many or too few for the number and ages of the children. There may be a lack of variety or not enough duplicate toys, leading to numerous conflicts between children. Toys and materials may remain the same from day to day and for weeks at a time, limiting infants' and toddlers' ways of learning.

In addition, there is often little provision made for individual needs within a group child care setting. Infants and toddlers in group care may be frustrated by adults who expect them to act as a group or who don't have the time or the skills to build relationships with individual children. There is often not enough space or appropriate equipment to foster the physical development of these very young children. Caregivers, in turn, are frustrated when their hard work and effort to "teach" is met with resistance or indifference. Practices such as these do not work for very young children. They reflect a lack of understanding of infants' and toddlers' emerging development and capabilities. They result in frustration for children and adults alike.

Materials are related to caregivers' interests rather than those of the children

Caregivers may choose toys and equipment that are cute or convenient for the caregiver rather than appealing to the children's curiosity. Infants and toddlers become frustrated or disengaged when toys are not relevant to their investigations. For example, an infant who is confined to "play"

in a swing is unable to move and explore her environment, or a toddler who doesn't have access to books or blocks is limited by a lack of hands-on experiences, even if there are alphabet letters emblazoned in the carpet or in murals.

Caregivers choose materials that can be used in only one way and restrict or limit their use

Infants and toddlers lose interest quickly when toys have limited play possibilities. For example, battery-operated toys do not allow a child to discover cause and effect. Pushing the rooster button on a See 'n Say toy will always result in the rooster sound. No matter what the child does with the toy, there is only one result, which does not encourage the child to investigate further. The possibilities for exploration of this type of material are limited because the ways it can be used are so few. Moreover, a child's curiosity is limited when caregivers restrict the inventive use of toys. For example, by not allowing small blocks to be used as pretend food in the play kitchen, a caregiver may unintentionally hinder a child's imaginative play. Similarly, a caregiver demonstrating that "Airplanes move like *this*" instead of asking "How do you think that airplane moves?" cuts a child's play short by supplying her with a "right" answer instead of encouraging her further observation and her own interpretation of what she sees.

All caregivers have to coordinate materials, time, themselves, and the children. Caregivers are lively, creative people, and sometimes they become so focused on their own expression that they forget about the interests of the children. Often, caregivers feel they must present something to entertain the children in order to feel in control. Parent expectations of a program may also put pressure on caregivers to provide a school-like curriculum. Themes or other teacher-driven principles are one way of organizing, but they tend to be fact-focused and adult-imposed instead of responsive to infants' and toddlers' immediate interests. Preschool type themes as organizational tools may work to focus caregivers, but do they work for infants and toddlers? What are infants and toddlers typically interested in? Consider the following scenario:

Summer is caregiver Wanda's favorite time of year. She is eager to share with this group of toddlers the wonders of caterpillars and butterflies. She has spent many nap times creating a bulletin board depicting them. It is late May in her northern city, and there has not yet been a butterfly for the children to see. During nap she was cutting paper into caterpillar and butterfly shapes for her painting project, but some toddlers woke up early and she couldn't finish her preparations. Twenty-six-month-old Romy doesn't even approach the table; he wanders the room. Two-year-olds Sam and Shana eagerly sit down to paint. After getting them started, Wanda quickly cuts a few more sheets for the next group. Shana reaches for the scissors. "No, today you are painting," Wanda tells Shana. "Remember how we talked about the caterpillars and butter-flies? There on the bulletin board," she points. Shana ignores the board, saying, "I wanna cut." Twenty-month-old Eric wanders off with a brush in his hand, and Wanda chases after him: "No, Eric. We are painting at the table." In the ensuing tussle to get Eric to the table, they both are spotted with paint, and Shana has retreated to suck her thumb by the door.

What do you think of this experience for both the caregiver and toddlers? Wanda's determination to follow her plan to present the caterpillar-to-butterfly lesson makes the painting process, in which the children are interested, incidental. Understanding that infants and toddlers learn from hands-on exploration would lead her to follow the children's interest. The multiple *no* directives the toddlers hear limit their exploration and use of the materials.

Children are expected to move through the day as a group because the environment is inflexible

It may seem efficient or logical to organize a child care center to use separate rooms or areas for specific functions —one room for play, another for eating, restrooms or diaper-changing areas for toileting. But the inflexibility inherent in this "school model" compromises infant/ toddler caregivers' efforts to meet individual needs. When children are expected to do everything on the same schedule, individual needs are not recognized nor met. Infants and toddlers forced to conform to an external schedule find it difficult to trust their own perceptions of when they are hungry or sleepy. An infant's task of learning trust is threatened when they are fed on a schedule that doesn't jibe with feeling hungry. Toddlers are frustrated when their expressions of self-concept are thwarted because caregivers cannot make provision for personal rhythms of eating, sleeping, or playing.

Children's interactions with one another are inhibited or even hurtful

Infants and toddlers are frustrated in their efforts to connect with one another when caregivers are unable or do not know how to support their desire to be social and play together. When caregivers provide too many toys in a disorganized manner, infants may be overwhelmed and unable to focus. Toddlers may launch into a nervous glee, running and throwing. When too few toys are available, infants and toddlers don't have the "lab equipment," as Alison Gopnik refers to it, that they need to run their experiments. For example, two toddlers may express their desire to play by grabbing at a single pull toy in the environment. Since it is the only one, their focus is changed from playing with the toy (the "experiment") to simply obtaining it at any cost, which often results in hitting, kicking, and crying.

Caregivers' interactions with children are perfunctory or controlling

When caregivers do not see themselves as an integral or inclusive part of the child's environment, they may interact with children in mechanical, impersonal ways. If an inappropriate environment causes infant/toddler play to repeatedly lead to unsafe situations, caregivers may see their job limited to keeping kids safe by controlling their behavior. This may take the form of using sharp verbal directives, or even various forms of physical restraint. Thus infants, toddlers, and their caregivers are denied the precious emotional and social connections that contribute to the children's learning and make the job satisfying for adults. Caregivers without developmental understanding may also have unrealistic expectations of infant/toddler capabilities.

The following two scenarios demonstrate in detail the missed connections arising when infants and toddlers are expected to move in groups or share too few materials. What happens when a child is not interested or refuses to participate with the group? What is the experience of this child and how does it affect others? The first scenario depicts what happens when a toddler is on a different eating schedule for that day and the play space is separate from the eating room.

It is lunchtime and twenty-seven-month-old Blaine refuses to stop his play to go to the eating room. Caregiver Eloise says to him, "Blaine, you have to come eat lunch now." Blaine yells no as Eloise picks him up, screaming. In the eating room, she puts Blaine down, still crying, as she helps the other children prepare to eat. Eloise says to her colleague Ned, "I don't know what to do with him—he won't come to the table." Ned responds, "I know, and we can't lose one of us to go back to the playroom with him." Eloise says to Blaine, "You have to eat now because it's time." Blaine wails, "No, I not hungry," as the other kids watch him, wide-eyed.

Notice in the scenario how the eating room is separate from the play space. Because Blaine has no opportunity to play while the others eat, his unhappy wailing makes the lunch experience very uncomfortable for all. The caregivers see Blaine as the problem, since he won't do what they want or what the program schedule dictates. What is Blaine learning from this experience? Probably that his feelings of not being hungry are disregarded and therefore unimportant. Over time, after a number of experiences like this, Blaine will learn to eat when he's not hungry and dismiss his own body's hunger signals.

Similarly, lack of developmentally based planning affects the toddlers' experiences in the next scenario.

Following their afternoon nap, six toddlers from eighteen to thirty months old enter a room with one caregiver, Jan. The room is open, with no dividers and two toy shelves against opposite walls. Twenty-eight-month-old Brenda picks up the tub of two dozen wooden blocks from the shelf, lifting them shoulder high, dumping them on the floor, and watching them bounce wildly. She smiles and begins walking among them, kicking each block. Nineteen-month-old Jill and twenty-month-old Tim get hit by the kicked blocks and begin crying, frozen to their spots, with their eyes shut tightly. Jan rushes to Jill and Tim, saying, "There, there. You're okay, don't cry," while reaching for Brenda, who continues to kick blocks. Meanwhile, at the other toy shelf, nine feet away, Julia and Ben, both two years old, fight over a bead-and-wire maze toy. "Mine," they each shout, leading to shoving, hitting, and crying. Jan is holding Brenda's hand and leads her over to Julia and Ben. Jan has to let go of Brenda in order to intervene with Julia and Ben. "If you won't play together, find something else to play with," she tells them. Brenda runs back to kick blocks, and Jan raises her voice to tell her, "Don't do that!" Eighteen-month-old Lena sits on a pillow in the corner sucking her thumb, clutching her blanket, and watching intently.

Notice how one large tub of too many blocks is used: the twenty-eight-month-old dumps them on the floor and ends up kicking blocks into other toddlers who are hurt by this action. Meanwhile, two two-year-olds grapple over a single maze toy, resulting in hurt and tears. The lack of duplicate toys results in two toddlers fighting over the single toy they are both interested in. All this overstimulates the youngest member of the large group to the point of wide-eyed withdrawal. The lack of environmental planning puts the caregiver in the position of having to solve too many problems (kicking the dumped blocks, two hurt children, conflict over the maze toy, and the obvious fear of the youngest child) at the same time. She would probably manage any one of these well, but it's not possible for her to cope with all of them at

once and serve the needs of all the children in the group.

Children's physical activity is limited

Infants and toddlers need to move vigorously in order to act on objects and explore the world. Caregivers who do not recognize the practice necessary to master small- and large-motor control will expect young children to move only at appointed times during the day. Children will find ways to exercise growing muscles even when appropriate venues are not available. For example,  toddlers will climb up to stand on anything at their waist height. Early crawlers will tackle stairs, and carefully practice their grasp on any small pieces of debris they find.

In the next scenario, the caregiver fails to account for the emerging physical development of the infants in her care. What do you think the experience of the infants is in this scene? What do you think they might be learning?

It is midmorning in the infant room. The caregiver, Muna, is caring for four infants four to ten months old. The floor is strewn with toys, so there is not a clear path in any direction. Four-month-old Maddie lies in the middle of the floor. Muna is sitting in the rocking chair giving a bottle to nine-month-old Kitty. Meanwhile, ten-month-old Ricky is crawling over Maddie, who begins crying, in an effort to pull up on his knees. He crawls past seven-month-old Edo, then over to pull up on Muna's knee in an effort to get vertical. Ricky leaves Maddie crying in his wake. Edo tries to scrabble after him through the toys.

Notice how four-month-old Maddie has no open floor space to practice rolling and is vulnerable where she is. Ricky has to crawl over Maddie to get to the caregiver in order to practice pulling up to a stand. Maddie cries in her frustration at this indignity. Kitty's intimate feeding time with her caregiver is interrupted. The lack of caregiver planning in this room limits the infants' opportunity for physical activity. Chaos and frustration ensue, and the children's basic safety is in jeopardy, as is the quality of care.

We have seen how infants and toddlers were frustrated in the previous scenarios, but what about the caregivers' experiences? Wanda's choice and use of materials reflect a lack of understanding the need to support infant/toddler curiosity. She wasn't able to share her interests as she had planned, and she probably felt as frustrated and disappointed about this as she felt exasperated at having her lesson interrupted and ignored.

Eloise, Ned, and Jan did not make the connections with the children that would have helped them enjoy their work. Because of the inflexibility of their environment, Ned and Eloise had an unpleasant lunchtime with a screaming child instead of a peaceful half hour with some children absorbed in lunch and one absorbed in play.

The lack of planning in Jan's toy selection created more conflict than she could reasonably handle—it's sure that she didn't enjoy this part of her day, and the after-nap incident quite likely set up an unhappy afternoon for several of the children, and for Jan as well.

Muna experienced a very frustrating morning because her space didn't provide the different kinds of supports that the infants in her care need to move in developmentally appropriate ways.

The caregivers in these scenarios work hard. They care about the children and try to do what's right for them. But the environments they work in are working *against* them. Unless these caregivers recognize the barriers to children's development in these environments, they will continue to be frustrated and surprised by children's response to their hard work. This feeling of being "at sea," without the anchor of developmental knowledge, will continue to damage their feelings of satisfaction on the job.

When Planning Is Sensitive to Children's Development

We've talked about the problems that occur when caregivers do not include infant/toddler development in planning the care environment. Now let's discuss how environments can support caregivers in meeting the developmental needs of infants and toddlers. We are suggesting ways to provide an environment in which infants and toddlers can engage themselves and safely do what they need to without waiting for

---

When planning is appropriate to infant and toddler development:

Materials are related to children's interests

Caregivers choose open-ended materials and encourage children's free exploration and experimentation

The environment is flexible and allows for individual schedules

The space supports children's play in small groups

Caregivers are free to respond calmly and interact warmly with children

Children's need to practice physical skills is honored

something to happen or for direction from caregivers. This is the vision!

Materials are related to children's interests

When caregivers use their knowledge of infant/toddler development to plan the environment, they know that there is a purpose underlying children's play. Planning is based on observation of the individual children and the group as a whole. For example, an infant who is squirming and reaching for her bottle or her caregiver's glasses is seeking hands-on experiences. The responsive caregiver will provide floor time for the infant to reach and move toward simple objects to mouth and investigate them. Caregivers who observe and listen to toddlers will recognize recurring themes of interest such as wanting to know how things work, their own impact on people and objects, daily life imitations, skill practice, family, peers, and the natural world. Related materials would include props for imitative and imaginative play, and manipulatives for building—and tearing down!

Caregivers choose open-ended materials and encourage children's free exploration and experimentation

Caregivers choose materials that lend themselves to multiple uses or are open-ended. The environment is set up so there's a free flow from area to area in order to encourage the possibility of using the materials in a new way. For example, "loose parts" are made available in an organized manner. Infants can crawl to the shelf to choose a rattle from an assortment of toys and carry it across the room and put it in the toy mailbox. Related toys in baskets line the shelves indoors, and crates of related toys are accessible to toddlers outdoors.

Remember Wanda, who loves the wonders of nature? This morning, twenty-two-month-old Shana discovered a bunch of sow bugs under some leaves, and they watched them together before going in to lunch. During nap time, Wanda found small magnifying glasses and some clear plastic containers. Instead of the painting she had planned to do as a small-group experience, they will observe the bugs. In addition to planning the bug experience, Wanda set up her room with related books and access to other materials for those children whose focus on the bugs may be short. Here's what Wanda's afternoon looks like now:

After nap and snack, Wanda invites four toddlers to join her in the yard. She provides them each with a clear plastic container and helps them gently gather leaves and sow bugs in the jars. Wanda adds ants to the experience when Eric expresses interest in the small moving insects. Indoors, she models using the magnifying glass to look at the bugs. "Big," Sam says, moving the glass back and forth over the bugs. "Yes, the bugs look bigger through the magnifying glass," Wanda says. This small-group experience offers opportunity for conversation. Eric comments, "Fast." Wanda responds, "Yes, their legs move quickly." Shana asks, "What doin'in?" Wanda replies, "What do you think they are doing?" "Crawling," "walking," "looking for some-

thing to eat," and "looking for their mommy" are some responses from the toddlers. Sam tries to hit the bugs with the magnifying glass, so Wanda suggests he look at a bug book, or pound on a pillow. After eight minutes of watching, twenty-six-month-old Romy says, "Me too," and comes into the circle to see the bugs.

Wanda is likely to have a much better afternoon following the children's interest in the sow bugs than she did when she proceeded with a project that came from her interest in caterpillars and butterflies. She is sustained by the deep connections resulting from responding to the children's interests. When she follows the children's interests, she is continually renewed by their discoveries and views of the world instead of spending a lot of her time managing their behavior.

The environment is flexible and allows for individual schedules

Each room or area can be set up to meet multiple needs of the children so that caregivers can find ways to honor individual schedules. Just as caregivers don't expect every thirteen-month-old to walk or every two-year-old to wear a size six shoe, they understand that children's day-to-day internal needs for rest or food may vary. (After all, they don't all poop at the same time!) It is important to each child's emotional development that caregivers plan an environment in order to predictably and consistently meet children's needs. Infants and toddlers are reassured by this respectful flexibility, especially when their internal clocks vary from the program schedule. The caregiver enhances his relationship with each child by building trust in this way; he makes connections, provides models for other children, and supports emotional development.

The space supports children's play in small groups

When caregivers commit to supporting infant/toddler social and emotional needs, their space is planned so that parallel or interactive play can take place without interruption from the flow of foot traffic. Efforts are made to provide many small areas for a few infants and toddlers to connect, rather than expecting eight or twelve toddlers to find each other in the large group. Within the planned spaces, multiples of the

same toys are available so that children can play together with minimal conflict. Toys and materials are organized in a way that creates a comfortable space for two to four infants or two to four toddlers to play.

Caregivers are free to respond calmly and interact warmly with children

Confident caregivers see themselves as an integral part of the children's environment. They recognize the value of having a connection with each child in order to support their learning. When a caregiver responds with a smile, a child feels that their expressions of learning are appreciated. For example, when two toddlers simultaneously grab for the same toy, the caregiver calmly responds, "I can tell you both want to play with that truck. Who's going to go get the other truck over there? Then you can play together." Caregivers who know infant/toddler development welcome conflict between children as a learning opportunity.

The following two scenarios demonstrate the power of changing the environment. Both Eloise and Jan found ways to make the environment work for the children as well as themselves.

First, let's revisit Eloise and Blaine, this time showing how the needs of all the children can be met even when one child may not be hungry at the scheduled lunchtime. Just as each child is on her own track of independent learning, her caregiving needs do not always occur at the same time as other children's nor on the center's schedule. Eloise brainstormed with other caregivers about this recurring problem and they decided to modify the environment so that each room can function independently to provide food, diapers, and choices of play objects. Let's see how it plays out.

As lunchtime approaches, the caregivers anticipate this for the playing toddlers: "In five minutes, it'll be time to go and get our hands washed for lunch."

Eloise remembers that two-year-old Blaine arrived only recently, because he had a late breakfast with his dad. She says to him, "I know you may not be hungry for lunch right now, but I need you to come in when we serve lunch to everyone else. You can find a truck inside, play dress up, or read books. You are welcome to join us for lunch or you can eat after your nap."

Note how Eloise responds to Blaine's individual needs for that day. Blaine can continue playing and the caregivers can maintain the ratio because there are play materials in the same room where meals are served. The other children are not distracted by any conflict, and all enjoy a tension-free lunch. Everyone's needs are met in a smooth, respectful manner.

Now let's see how Jan might respond to toddlers Brenda, Julia, Ben, Jill, Tim, and Lena. Six toddlers with one caregiver is not an optimum ratio, but developmental planning by the caregiver can make even a difficult situation much better.

After the block-kicking incident, Jan planned to alter the environment. First, she divided the blocks into two baskets for dumping and filling. She added two baskets of soft balls as safe throwing and kicking alternatives for the toddlers. She put away the single maze toy, and placed two large barns in an area with two baskets of farm animals next to them. She checked to be sure there were books near one pillow and baby dolls with blankets near another.

When the toddlers enter the room after their naps, they discover a new scene. Twenty-eight-month-old Brenda immediately dumps out one basket of blocks, and Jan points out that she can dump them from one basket to the other. Ben runs to the farm setup. He chooses a cow, and Julia grabs it. Jan shows Julia that there are two baskets with the same animals: "Julia, you can have this basket with a cow, or you can offer to trade cows. Ben has this one. Look, now you each have a horse and a cow." They move to put the cows in the barns. Brenda looks up and tosses a block, never breaking her gaze on Jan. "Here's a safe thing to throw," Jan says as she starts a game of catch with Brenda, using the soft balls. Nineteen-month-old Jill heads right for the baby dolls, "Here, here," she says as she hands one to Tim, who is twenty months old. Lena comes in dragging her blanket and goes to wake up gradually on a pillow.

Notice that the changes in the environment do not eliminate infant/toddler testing behaviors. The changes do provide safe and okay alternatives, reflecting an understanding of infant/toddler development. The environment supports the caregiver in the use of the strategies for caring interactions. When the toddlers are settled in the environment, each child is comfortably doing what they need to with an engaged caregiver nearby.

Children's need to practice physical skills is honored

As caregivers understand that each child is on his own developmental path—from infancy on—they plan an environment that offers many opportunities for children to negotiate their relationship with gravity and space. For example, infants need open floor space to practice rolling over and developing the muscles that will support them when sitting up by themselves. Self-feeding O's breakfast cereal is an opportunity to practice their pincer grasp. Toddlers benefit from using crayons or markers to develop their finger grasp and control for future experiences involving scissors and writing. Children are at liberty to practice coordination wherever they find themselves because provisions for both large- and small-motor practice have been made

both indoor and out. Caregivers are careful to provide alternative places to climb, soft objects that are okay to throw indoors, and small implements for sand and water outdoors. Practice climbing, running, and riding trikes enables toddlers to increase the breadth of their curious explorations and integration of skills.

The reason caregivers need to understand child development is that it alters their planning. When caregivers know what behaviors to expect, they can set up the environment to match the developmental needs of each child in their care. Let's revisit Muna to see how she sets up the environment to meet the needs of Maddie, Edo, Ricky, and Kitty in the infant room.

Before her infants arrive the next morning, Muna puts three baskets of toys on the floor: one with balls, one with rattles, and one with board books. Edo, seven months, and Kitty, nine months, will enjoy crawling around to find the different sensorial rolling and sound-making toys in the baskets. She leaves some open floor space because she knows four-month-old Maddie will want to practice rolling over. Muna pulls a sturdy low table to one end of the room, because she's observed ten-month-old Ricky trying to pull up to a stand. She arranges pillows and cushions so that Edo and Kitty are challenged to crawl over an obstacle. She also plans a place for herself on the floor to be available while giving each their bottles. Muna begins this day confident that it will be more enjoyable for all.

We have pointed out how both ineffective and functional environments directly affect the development of infants and toddlers and the satisfaction of the caregiver. Caregivers who learn to plan environments as Wanda, Eloise,

Jan, and Muna did will be able to stem the tide of demands and participate with the children in the flow of their day-to-day development. Their efforts will make a huge difference in the growth and learning of the children who are in their care, and their days will be much more enjoyable too!

Planning an Environment to Meet Developmental Needs

We know caregivers want to do the best job they can for the children in their care. When caregivers find themselves frustrated by recurring situations, they may find they are unable to support the development of each child in their care. For example, caregivers may find themselves

- repeatedly reacting to physical aggression by the children;
- repeating directions many times to children who are unresponsive;
- faced with more than one child in a group who is inconsolably upset.

We will suggest a process that can help caregivers discover how environmental barriers cause frustration. Often these barriers prevent children from doing what comes naturally.

Begin planning the environment by observing the individual children in your group. Observation allows the caregiver to see the real fourteen-month-old in front of her instead of the theoretical one from a book or chart. The trick is for caregivers to know child development *and* accept individual differences; to see individual maturation instead of expecting all children who are the same age to be doing the same things. This is particularly important in group care so

that caregivers allow for these individual differences in their planning.

In order to plan an environment that meets the needs of infants and toddlers, caregivers who work together can use the following process. Be sure that licensing, health, and safety regulations are met throughout the planning.

1. Evaluate the environment

2. Decide what to change

3. Choose materials and consider how they are presented and arranged

4. Observe how the new environment is used by children and adults (and modify as needed by repeating steps 1–3)

1. Evaluate the environment

Use the following questions to guide your evaluation of an environment. Each caregiver can make notes to answer the questions. Focus on what the children are really doing in the environment rather than what is supposed to happen.

What interests, actions, and interactions does the environment support? For example, are children's curiosities or interests supported? How? Does the environment encourage children to make connections with one another and their caregivers? How? Can the children move physically in the environment to gain coordination? What can an infant or toddler learn in this environment? How does the environment give children opportunities to make legitimate choices?

How does the arrangement of materials and equipment invite hands-on exploration? Are materials accessible to and easily used by

infants and toddlers? Can they build or manipulate objects and materials away from traffic areas? Is there space for push and pull toys? Are there duplicates of toys so children can explore freely?

How does the environment support caregivers in providing for flexible schedules to meet children's needs? Are play materials and eating materials available in the same space? Is there a place where a drowsy toddler can curl up for a nap?

How does the space support infants and toddlers playing safely together? Does the space support play in small groups through the arrangement of toys and equipment? Are there duplicates of toys so that two toddlers can play side by side or with each other? Are the numbers of children in any space conducive to playing in small groups?

Does the space support caregivers' being with the children? Are there comfortable places for adults to sit and be available to the children? Do caregivers have what they need in the space, or do they frequently have to step out of the space to attend to necessary chores?

How does the space support children's need for physical movement? What can infants and toddlers do or practice without interruption? Can they roll, crawl, walk, throw, climb, jump? Is there space to focus on small muscle coordination? Do the environments have traffic flow patterns that leave room for children to move without being in the middle of the traffic?

When you've answered these questions, you'll have a good idea of what's working in your environment. You may also already have some ideas of what to change. Now go back through these questions, and instead of asking "how does . . . " ask yourself "how could . . . "

For example, ask yourself, "How could the environment support children's following their interests? How could it encourage connections between children? How could it offer children legitimate choices?" and so forth.

2. Decide what to change

Observation coupled with the answers to the previous questions will tell caregivers what elements of the environment need to be changed. Making one change at a time will help caregivers see the effect of the change and decide if it works. One good place to start is the basic room arrangement and its relation to the traffic flow.

If some children are building with Duplo blocks and others have to step through or over them, the room arrangement or traffic flow is faulty. Caregivers can rearrange the area so the floor space for focused toddler play is out of the line of traffic between doorways or access to lofts or steps. The room arrangement can help infants and toddlers focus on specific tasks they seek to do. Toy shelves, small housekeeping furniture, pillows, couches, and hanging curtains could all be used to physically and visually define areas of play.

3. Choose materials and consider how they are presented and arranged

An appropriate variety of materials engages individuals and small groups as infants and toddlers focus on specific tasks. If toys and materials are being used inappropriately or in unsafe ways, caregivers can remind themselves that a child's behavior is the expression of need. Follow these simple steps to choose materials:

Decide which toys to make available, based on previous observations.

For example:

- Has there been a lot of inappropriate throwing?

     You may want to supply safe things for children to throw and games that involve them in appropriate throwing.

- Can they never get enough of a certain toy, such as trains?

     You might consider bringing out toy trains (both miniature ones and riding toys), dress-up clothes that will support children's train-related dramatic play, and books about trains.

- Have they stopped noticing certain objects, like the mobile?

     Maybe it's time to change to new ones, or move them to different places in the room.

Consider how to organize and arrange the toys so they suggest exploration to the children. The more organized an area is, the more organized play is for toddlers. When a room or area is a mess, resulting play tends to be chaotic, as toddlers rush from toy to toy and idea to idea or are interrupted by others.

Presenting materials in an organized manner allows children to focus on a specific task or idea. Separate areas can be set up with materials for toddlers to practice specific skills, such as pulling, filling and dumping, climbing, and putting together. It is important to provide multiples of larger toys such as barns, garages, and wheeled vehicles so toddlers can play side by side or together with the same toys. Baskets help to organize smaller manipu-

latives so that toddlers can categorize and carry them around.

It's important for caregivers to provide toddlers with materials and space to play so all their intended behaviors are okay or have an acceptable alternative that fulfills their expressed need.

Consider the overall group size. How many children at a time use which spaces, and what is the developmental range in these groups? Will you need duplicates or even triplicates of the same toys? Group size is one of the most important factors influencing the behaviors and interactions of children in an environment. The larger the group, the easier it is for infants and toddlers to get overwhelmed or overstimulated, and the less opportunity children will have for friendly interactions with one another. At the same time, a critical mass is necessary for children to interact at all. Even if there is enough space and adequate supervision for each child to have her own little cubby and enough of every toy for each child to have her own, the children wouldn't learn much about how to be with one another. Small groups of two to four children are most effective for supporting social interaction among infants and toddlers.

One way to use available space for all the play needs in a group is to plan interest centers or *pockets of play*. Pockets of play attract infants and toddlers into small groups in small, defined areas within a larger environment. Young children are naturally drawn to one another. Infants and toddlers seek one another out to imitate, interact with, and play nearby. Caregivers can present, arrange, and separate areas of play to encourage small-group interactions. Each area, or "pocket," presents related materials that may suggest a basis of play. Be delighted when they take the idea and run!

For example, an outdoor area is used by three caregivers and twelve toddlers every morning and afternoon. There are some permanent structures, areas of grass and sand, and a concrete

A basket of balls is set next to a rigid tunnel, which today is set at an angle safely supported by tires. Each of these pockets is self-contained, although the toddlers may transport objects between them. There are baskets of hats, balls, shovels and pails, and pull toys available to the toddlers. A board is set at an angle leading to the ladders to the loft and the slide. When toddlers spill into the yard after their naps, each child will be able to discover a pocket of play that appeals to her. Because each small area is well defined, toddlers are likely to end up in small groups of two to four children, rather than in one big clump.

If this yard also must accommodate three or four infants, special planning needs to occur. Placing the babies in the yard requires consideration of shade, sun, and vulnerability to the movements of older children. For instance, it is often fascinating for babies to be under trees and watch the leaves move, where they are also protected from the sun; near grass or other different textures; or near a wind chime or streamer. Planning a safe space for immobile babies involves consideration of what caregivers know will occur. Toddlers love babies and their special toys, so caregivers can plan to respond accordingly. One idea could be to provide baby dolls for toddlers to act out their interest, imitating the caregiver caring for the babies.

circular path. Portable equipment includes slides; snap-together wall blocks; picnic tables; push, pull, and wheeled toys; trikes; and sand toys. Children can choose by pocket, peer, or caregiver where they want to be in the environment. Here's an example of how one caregiver set up pockets of play in this setting.

Caregiver Terry is responsible for the yard, and she has set it up so that the children can experience angles. Two large pieces of plywood set on a railroad tie buried in the sand form a ramp for wheeled toys. Four small trikes are arranged in a line close by. A fabric tunnel has been secured with a long, smooth board (12 by 10 feet) through it and then set onto a slanted mat, providing an angled, enclosed crawling and spatial experience. Soft cushions against a fence and a mat on the ground under the trees provide a quiet book area. Familiar sand toys are arranged in the play kitchen and by the table and chairs.

Think like an infant or a toddler. Remember that you are part of the environment too. How you respond to the infants and toddlers is the most important factor in the quality of their care. As you think about planning the environment and responding to the infants and toddlers you work with, we encourage you to think like an infant or toddler. When caregivers think like an infant or toddler, they move beyond the reactive response of saying no to an understanding response that offers a child an acceptable way to do what they need to do.

For example, infants and toddlers need to chew or bite. They sometimes choose other children for this need, which is not okay. Rather than saying, "No, don't do that," the caregiver can acknowledge the need to bite by providing a teether to the child: "I can't let you bite your friend; here's a teether to bite on" or "I can't let you chew the book, but you can bite on this teether." If the biting is in response to a conflict with another child, caregivers can help the child express his feeling using language like, "I know you really want that truck, but I can't let you bite your friend," and then giving the child words to use in the situation, such as: "Say, 'Mine; your

turn next.'" Biting is often a child's response to the pain of teeth growing in or a preverbal frustration when a child does not yet have the words to use. It is a behavior caregivers can expect to see in group child care. Similarly, other challenging actions are really movements that infants and toddlers naturally do and need to practice: climbing, hitting, pushing, throwing.

When caregivers can respond to children by allowing them to do what they need to do, caregivers are more relaxed and able to respond in an understanding way. Refer to the "Think Like an Infant/Toddler" chart on the next page for ideas about what to provide and how to respond so the infants and toddlers in your care can satisfy their curious investigations, make respectful connections with others and learn to resolve conflict, and practice coordination.

When caregivers learn to think like an infant or toddler, their expectations of children's behavior become realistic. Their response to children changes from punitive discipline to facilitation of learning. This relaxed, supportive response alleviates children's frustrations, and in turn it makes life easier for their caregivers!

As simple and obvious as the responses in the chart may appear, it takes commitment to consistently and respectfully follow through with children. Caregivers who practice this most creative aspect of caring for children will be rewarded by finding appropriate responses that also work for everyone in the program. A change in expectation is the key. When caregivers change their expectations of infants and toddlers, the door of possibility opens.

4. Observe how the new environment is used by children and adults (and modify as needed by repeating steps 1–3)

Take the time to sit and watch the children in the new environment. What is really happening? What are the children actually doing with the

Think Like an Infant/Toddler

Child's Behavior	Child's Developmental Need	Caregiver Provides
dumping/filling	cause and effect (predicting how objects move) power, control	multiple baskets and contents for filling/dumping
screaming indoors	cause and effect (observing the response) vocal experimentation	other vocal experiments such as "whisper scream," singing echo experience in bucket
pouring out beverage	understand properties of liquids finished eating or drinking	pouring pitcher to self serve more water play language to say "all done"
hitting/running or grabbing/running	explore own interests in own time play next to or with peer	duplicate or multiple toys scripts for turn taking and trading affirmation of mutual interests
pinching	pincer-grasp control making connections with others	more self-feeding practice alternative small-muscle experiences words to say (scripts), e.g., "Hi"
chewing/biting	exploring objects in environment teething relief	provide for clean and safe mouthing by rotating/cleaning toys teethers in every room
pulling hair	cause and effect (observing the response) connection	alternative cause-and-effect experiments scripts to help children connect gentle modeling
clinging	connection, trust	access to lap and/or lovey
crying	communication	empathy by acknowledging feelings
spitting	body awareness	alternatives of closing lips, saying "patooey!" or blowing kisses permission to spit outdoors in bushes or away from people
whining	communication	words to say in regular voice

Think Like an Infant/Toddler (continued)

Child's Behavior	Child's Developmental Need	Caregiver Provides
pushing	large-muscle skill practice making connection	carts or large balls to push offer other ways to use hands, say hi friendly scripts
throwing heavy toys	large-muscle or eye-hand coordination practice	soft things to throw indoors clear limits about what can be thrown a variety of balls outdoors
climbing on tables	large-muscle skill practice	appropriate places to climb: loft, stairs, couch
jumping on furniture	large-muscle skill practice	safe place for jumping
running indoors	large-muscle exuberance	marching indoors safe place for running outdoors
kicking toys or children	large-muscle skill practice	soft objects, okay to kick indoors balls outdoors
"belly flopping," e.g., on table or on other children	negotiating space, feeling powerful full-body contact/connection	appropriate space: waist-level flat surfaces such as cube chairs big pillows

space and materials? For example, are the children focused and engaged? Is there less conflict among children? Are caregivers available to support children's play? Are the materials being used safely or in ways that support children's growth and exploration? Do the changes in behavior match those expected from the changes made in the environment?

Modifications in the environment have to be made almost continually. Over the long term, as the developmental needs of each child changes, the toys that are available will look different and present new challenges for the children. (Remember "optimal stress"?) Planning for the

real behaviors and anticipating changing play needs of infants and toddlers allows the caregiver to relax and *be* with the children.

Other opportunities to modify the environment present themselves daily—sometimes even hourly! A caregiver may observe an individual or small group showing an increased interest in a particular task or specific objects of play. For example, when a caregiver observes that an infant is particularly curious about, say, noisemakers today, she can respond by modifying the environment to include a wider variety of objects that can make noise. Similarly, when one or several toddlers are putting all the available pop

Is the child's risk worth the learning that can occur?

To answer these questions, caregivers can look to their developmental knowledge of infants and toddlers. For example, if a caregiver observes a fourteen-month-old toddler standing on the open edge of a milk crate while holding onto a railing, the caregiver may need to redirect her to use the crate safely by turning it over, which still provides the opportunity for the child to fulfill her need to climb to a higher plane. On the other hand, when a two-and-a-half-year-old does the same thing, the caregiver can acknowledge her action as a test of her coordination and an expression of her competence at balancing. Standing next to the toddler to "spot" her may still be necessary, but knowing the individual's capabilities will help the caregiver determine when and how much to spot or support a child's innovative use of materials. The key is to observe, support, and facilitate what infants and toddlers are trying to do rather than demanding that they do what a caregiver expects them to do.

beads or Duplo blocks together, an observant caregiver knows that their play possibilities will be expanded if they have more materials. She can respond to this focused play by pulling out more pop beads or Duplo blocks from storage. Remember, play equals learning!

As part of evaluating the physical environment, caregivers can pay attention to their own responses to children's exploration with the new materials or room arrangement. They can ask themselves:

What is this child learning from my response?

Will the infant or toddler learn that their caregiver is frustrated or angry, or will the child learn what is okay to do by being offered a choice?

Does my response best meet the needs of this child at this time?

How is my response influenced by the environmental setup?

Given space and time to play freely, children will often discover innovative ways to play or manipulate objects. If a caregiver's first impulse is to intervene and stop the new manner of play, we suggest that the caregiver ask herself the following questions:

What is the worst that can happen?

What is the best that can happen?

Planned Experiences for Infants and Toddlers

Planned Experiences for Small Groups

We have tried to offer caregivers a strong foundation for evaluating and planning an environment that supports infant/toddler learning and respectful caregiver response. We have also discussed the benefits of providing for small groups of infants and toddlers within a group care setting. Now we will explain how caregivers can plan experiences for small groups of infants and toddlers that focus on their areas of development: curiosity, connection, and coordination.

Experience or activity?

We prefer to use the word *experience* to describe the kinds of things we do with children, because to us, *activity* implies an end product, while *experience* focuses on the process of exploring. One way to determine what qualifies as an experience rather than an activity is to pay attention to how much caregivers rely upon saying *no* and *don't* to the infants and toddlers. Remember Wanda and her caterpillar-to-butterfly activity? If you have to work to keep the children focused on what you want or intend them to do with the materials, as Wanda did, what children experience is frustration and probably the caregiver's tension as well. Infants and toddlers are learning *how* to learn and that their learning is based on exploration and experimentation rather than direction from others.

An activity like Wanda's is usually too rigid for infants and toddlers. Social connections are stifled when young children have to listen to the caregiver instead of interact with their peers. Caregivers are unable to facilitate interactions when they are intent on giving directions. Since infants and toddlers are hands-on learners, restricting the innovative use of materials actually keeps them from learning.

What is a planned experience?

During a planned experience of the kind we suggest, caregivers set up materials for use by small groups of infants, toddlers, or infants and toddlers together (usually for a total of four children in a group). The small group provides for more

able to reflect or participate, responding to the lead of the children. From the close observation that this kind of environment affords, caregivers can choose or create related planned experiences that extend the children's interest.

Ari, August, Jim, and Phillip, all two-year-old toddlers, are playing together indoors. They are playing informally in a room with housekeeping items set up under a loft, shelves for other toys, large tables for serving meals, and a soft area with books close by. They are reenacting a picnic birthday party they all attended over the weekend.

"Come, come over here," August invites the others. They carry dishes from the kitchen area under the loft to the table. They sit across from each other as at a picnic table. "We're having a picnic," Jimmy informs the caregiver, Vanessa. "Oh?" she responds. "We have juice and hamburgers," Phillip offers. Ari follows, carrying a plate carefully. He sits next to Phillip, grinning. "Juice," he repeats, taking the cup from Phillip. August is busy passing out plates: "You want? You want?" He and Jimmy pretend to eat for one minute. Phillip begins to try to balance the juice bottle on his head. Ari laughs, and Phillip tries again. Vanessa moves in closer. "You're trying to balance that bottle on your head," she comments, "Maybe we can try balancing later, after lunch and nap. In two minutes it will be time to clean up for lunch." Jimmy bursts into action, stacking dishes in his arms to carry to the kitchen area. "Whoa, Jimmy!" Vanessa observes, "You are balancing lots of dishes in your arms! It's okay, Ari, you can play for two more minutes."

personal interaction between the children and the caregiver and among the children. It also allows the caregiver to notice what individual children are interested in and provide support for interactions among the children. Many of the experiences in this book revolve around art, such as painting, gluing, and drawing with markers. Others take an idea and support infants or toddlers in investigating it. Observations made during small-group planned experiences may have implications for the overall environmental setup. Infant/toddler interests and skills that go unnoticed in large groups reveal themselves in small-group interactions. Caregivers can use this information to plan further experiences or to alter the overall environment.

We have tried to write a guide that weaves the caregiver strategies into the planned experiences with the developmental tasks of infants and toddlers in mind. We want to provide opportunities for children to learn through investigation, rather than fuel the old paradigm of caregivers feeling a need to entertain them.

How to Choose a Planned Experience

In the following example, the environment is set up for child-initiated play. The caregiver is avail-

Vanessa notes that balancing is a skill Phillip and Jimmy want to investigate. She can be ready after nap with small boxes or blocks to make balancing practice safe. (See "Balancing Practice" on page 106.) It will be interesting to see if Phillip and Jimmy remember their earlier interest or if it was just a passing fancy. Vanessa might plan to offer the balancing experience for a few days and revisit it in a couple of weeks. Another experience related to their play might be cooking. Toddlers are capable of simple cooking projects and enjoy them as something "real." (See "Making Pudding" on page 137.)

How to Use the Planned Experiences

The experiences in the following section are organized by developmental age: Infant (for those children not yet walking), Infant/Toddler (for older infants and younger toddlers), and Toddler (for those older toddlers whose mastery of the basics allows them to use materials innovatively or to investigate new possibilities).

Each experience has a brief description, list of materials, procedures, and other things to think about. A scenario describing a real interaction during each experience will help caregivers anticipate how it might go in their own program. We have tried to give the sound and feel of the

actual experience in the belief that this will be most helpful to new caregivers or to caregivers trying an experience for the first time.

Many of the experiences are flexible enough to be used inside or outside and may be adapted for rainy days. Many use common materials. Necessary setup and cleanup time is included for involving the children in smooth transitions.

We recognize the time and commitment it takes to be comfortable carrying out this kind of planning, *and* we know the rewards of doing what is right and respectful for each child. Have fun too!

Planned Experiences

Colored Cellophane on a Sunny Window

Placing colored cellophane on a window where sunlight shines through makes a colored light that infants can discover and notice as it moves with the sun across the room.

What You'll Need

- Various colors of cellophane.
- Clear tape.
- Sunlight through a window, or another source of light to shine through the cellophane.
- Clear Con-Tact paper and white paper to make a permanent viewing spot on the floor or shelf.

What to Do

- Cut cellophane into approximately 12-inch-square pieces.
- Determine where the sunlight falls on the floor or wall and where the cellophane needs to be on the window to make the light colored for the maximum amount of time during the day.
- Tape the cellophane squares to the window.
- Allow infants to discover the new type of sunlight on their own.

Limits

- Cellophane is best placed out of the reach of children (they will naturally pull it down).

Other Things to Think About

- Overlapping primary colors of cellophane in the order red, yellow, blue will produce the secondary colors orange and green. To make purple, overlap the red and blue.

- Some shelves have pegboard backing with small holes in it; cover the holes with colored cellophane where light will come through. To make it easier to see the colored light on the shelves, attach white paper to the shelves with clear Con-Tact paper.

Supporting Play

Use these strategies, shown in the following scenario, to support children's play:

- Validate child's experience.

- Share caregiver's interests ("Say who you are").

Nine-month-old William is crawling on the rug, patting the red color coming through the cellophane with the palm of his hand, then crawling to another color. He looks back at caregiver Joe. "You found the colors on the floor," Joe comments. "That one is red like your shirt." William rocks back on his bottom. Holding up his hand, he waves it through the red light. "See your hand?" Joe asks. "The light is pretty fun, huh?" Later, after his nap and when the light is lower, William pulls up on a shelf. Discovering the colored holes on the back of the shelf, he turns to Joe, "Uh yi!" "Yes, you found more colored lights!" Joe says. William pounds on the shelf, steadying himself with the other hand.

Peekaboo Scarf

A picture of a face or familiar object covered by a scarf is mounted where babies can lift the scarf to play a peekaboo game.

What You'll Need

- Picture or photo of a familiar object or human or animal face.
- Scarf to cover the picture or photo.
- Tape.

What to Do

- Sew or tape the scarf to the picture. Or mount the picture on the wall and attach the scarf to the wall above the picture.
- Mount the picture where the babies can move the scarf themselves to see the picture behind it.

Limits

- If toddlers are participating, they may need to be reminded to leave the scarf over the picture so the babies can play too.

Other Things to Think About

- If the babies lose interest in this experience, substitute a different picture. For example, it could be an animal, members of their own families, or you could use their own picture.
- Multiple pictures could be displayed side by side and covered by the scarf.
- A mirror could be covered in the same way for a peekaboo game.

Supporting Play

Infants love controlling the repeated discovery in this game. Use these strategies, shown in the following scenario, to support children's play:

- Validate child's experience ("Say what you see").

Eleven-month-old Puna stops crawling in front of a scarf hanging on the end of the toy shelf. It wasn't there yesterday. She sits for thirty seconds, gazing at the plain scarf. Caregiver Angela looks up to see her there. "I see you noticed there's a scarf hanging there," she comments. Puna crawls on to get a squeeze toy off the shelf. Chewing on it makes it squeak, and Puna laughs out loud, dropping the toy. Crawling after it brings her back to the scarf. Puna grabs the bottom edge and crawls, pulling the scarf sideways. Now she can see the happy baby face underneath the scarf. Angela says, "You found the baby!" Puna stops to lift the scarf higher, drops it back over the picture, then uncovers it again. "Peekaboo," Angela says, and Puna repeats, "Boo."

Everything Has a Name!

Some time in the latter part of their first year, infants realize that everything has a name. Caregivers can recognize when this occurs and respond to the infant's expression of interest in learning language.

What You'll Need

No materials needed for this experience.

What to Do

- Listen for the "What's that?" question, which is sometimes accompanied by pointing, that many babies use to ask the names of things. This may take many forms, but it is special to each individual. Some examples are "Whatsit?" "Dat?" "Der," and "Wha?"

- Name the item for the baby, reflecting any attempts to say the word.

Limits

None needed.

Other Things to Think About

- Later on, the baby will ask "Whatsit?" as a tool to get the adult to ask him the question, because now he knows the name!

- Consider the environment in light of this new development. Plan to extend collections of familiar pictures to help infants recognize categories. Use pictures of differing cows, cats, or bears, for example.

Supporting Play

Use these strategies, shown in the following scenario, to support children's play:

- Honor communication and respond to child-initiated interactions.

Caregiver Polle speaks clearly about things that she and eleven-month-old Sunita are both seeing in the environment. For over a month, Sunita has been paying special attention to Polle's "sportscasting." Today, Sunita initiates the exchange by pointing at a picture of a dog mounted on the end of a toy shelf, saying, "Da?" "Dog, that's a dog," Polle answers. Sunita is kneeling in front of the mounted photos. She points at the next one, repeating, "Da?" Polle responds, "Cat." Sunita bounces on her knees and points again. "Oh, Fuzz! Your cat is named Fuzz," Polle says. Nodding and saying, "Uss, uss," Sunita crawls around the shelf.

Frozen Fruits and Vegetables

Teething babies appreciate the cold of frozen peas or blueberries as an addition to their meals. The cold, hardness, and rolling action makes it a multisensory experience. This experience points out overlapping processes of routine, play, and emerging development.

What You'll Need

- Permission from parents. Ask them to try these foods with their children at home first to be sure that the babies are not allergic to them.

- Frozen blueberries or peas in bowl.

- Bibs (blueberries may stain clothes).

What to Do

- At snack or meal times, spoon a few blueberries or peas onto the table in front of the infants, along with other finger food.

- Observe infants' reactions and validate their experience verbally ("Say what you see").

Limits

- Food is not for throwing.

Other Things to Think About

- Extend to include other frozen or cold fruits and vegetables, guided by the infants' preferences.

Supporting Play

Use these strategies, shown in the following scenario, to support children's play:

- Validate child's experience ("Say what you see").
- Promote self-awareness.

Nine-month-old Viviana and eleven-month-old Georgia are sitting at a table having lunch. Both have been chewing teethers all morning, so caregiver Lisa decides to offer frozen peas as part of lunch. She spoons out about a tablespoon or so for each infant. Viviana easily uses a pincer grasp to pick up a pea. She holds it up in front of her face and looks at it before putting it in her mouth. Now she is obviously chewing harder. "What do you think, Viviana?" Lisa says. Viviana quickly gets more peas. "Ama mo," she says. "I see you like the peas," says Lisa. Georgia picks up a pea and holds it fifteen seconds before pushing it into her mouth with her thumb. Lisa can see it against her cheek. "Look how you can pick up that pea. Do you feel how cold it is?" says Lisa. "Ah he do," Georgia says. Now she picks up one pea in each hand. "Ti di ti," Georgia says.

Mirrors

Placing various mirrors where mobile and nonmobile infants can see them engages infants with images of themselves and others.

What You'll Need

- Mirrors made of plastic/acrylic. (Mirrors may be mounted on cabinets, walls, or the floor. They are also a common element on infant toys.)

What to Do

- Seed the environment with mirrors. For example, permanently mount them at a low level on shelves or walls and on available toys.
- Watch for babies' interest. Allow them to discover mirrors on their own.
- Add other mirrors as interest increases, for example, next to the eating area or changing area.
- Respond to eye contact, perhaps by "entering" the mirror so your image is seen by the baby.

Limits

- No banging, even though these mirrors are plastic (not all the mirrors the children come into contact with will be plastic).
- Provide safe alternatives for hitting and banging.

Other Things to Think About

- Watch for recognition of self and others.
- Place mirrors at various heights to engage infants who are pulling up or cruising.
- Put some mirrors vertically, some horizontally, some diagonally.

Supporting Play

Use these strategies, shown in the following scenario, to support children's play:

- Validate child's experience ("Say what you see").

- Promote self-awareness.

Nena helps to enhance the children's connections with one another by placing the mirror where DJ and Ben can see each other while eating a meal together. The infants also each develop a sense of self by viewing their own images in the mirror.

Five-month-old DJ lies on the floor by a mirror. Turning his head and body toward the mirror, he catches sight of himself and holds his position, lying on his side. "Ah dah oooh," he says, smiling and gazing intently at the image. His right hand reaches toward the mirror and pulls back. "Ha!" he says loudly. Caregiver Nena says, "Oh, you saw your hand move in the mirror." Meanwhile, eleven-month-old Ben pulls up on the railing in the infant room. There is a mirror mounted at rail height. He smiles and mugs in the mirror, moving his mouth exaggeratedly and vocalizing, stopping to look into the mirror and smile every thirty seconds or so. "I see you making funny faces, Ben," Nena says. When it is time to eat, Nena holds DJ on her lap at the table while Ben feeds himself finger food. There is a long mirror on the wall next to the table, and Ben watches himself chew in the mirror.

Sensory Immersion

For full-body investigation of such properties as shape and texture, small wading pools can be used to hold items that babies can immerse themselves in.

What You'll Need

- Small (24-by-36-inch) wading pools (one for two babies, or two pools for three or four babies).

- A collection of similar items to fill the pools. For example, juice can lids, fabric pieces, balls, or small stuffed animals that also make noise. You might also consider a collection of related materials, such as several different kinds of balls.

What to Do

- Set up two wading pools for three to four infants to investigate. Having two allows comparison of the contents and movement between them.

- Fill each pool with a different collection of items, such as juice can lids in one and fabric or fur pieces in the other. Fill tubs so that the whole bottom of the pool is covered or to a depth of approximately one to two inches, depending on the material.

- Mirror sounds, words, comments, and other reactions that babies make as they move through, taste, rub, and otherwise experience the contents of the pools.

- Plan for washing the materials used, since they will be mouthed and drooled on!

Limits

- If used outdoors, plan for keeping materials in one place.

Other Things to Think About

- How can you plan for use outdoors?

- How can you plan for multiage use?

- Extend the experience by using the same materials in another way and in a different place in the room. For example, use juice can lids as a shape-sorting toy by dropping them into the slit top of a coffee can. (See "Infant Shape Sorter," p. 72.)

Supporting Play

Use these strategies to support children's play, as shown in the following story:

- Validate child's experience ("Say what you see").

- Offer information ("Say what you know").

Caregiver Nadia has set up two pools—one full of juice can lids, and one full of pieces of sheepskin and fake fur. Upon arrival, each baby discovers the pools. Ten-month-old Kanisa crawls to and easily climbs into the tub with the lids. Her eyebrows up and her mouth smiling, she uses both hands to sweep through the lids. Coming up grasping lids in each hand, she bangs them together, singing a varied pitch vocalization: "Hm-ha, hm-ham, da da dahhhhhh." "I hear you making music, Kanisa," Nadia comments. Eight-month-old Peter belly-flops into the pool with the sheepskin. He's grinning, reaching out to grasp and pull a piece to his face. He buries his face in it like a dog shaking a toy. "Oh, do you like the soft sheepskin?" Nadia asks. "Here's a piece with the skin side up. What do you think?" Later, when these two children have their nap, Nadia places five-month-old Ronald in the pool with the sheepskin. Wriggling around, he settles onto the soft but uneven surface. Flailing his arms, he pats a piece of fur. "It's soft," Nadia says.

Texture Mat

Beginning crawlers will experience different sensations under their hands and feet as they move along a path of varying textures. This experience provides an opportunity for caregivers to use descriptive language to reflect the infants' reactions to the materials.

What You'll Need

- Squares or other shapes of varying textured materials: velvet, corduroy, fake fur, pieces of vinyl, stiff interfacing, large buttons (sewn on securely), one side of a strawberry basket (with edges smoothly covered and securely sewn on), a fabric bag filled with aquarium rock, textured shelf liner, Velcro (both hook and loop sides), sandpaper, and bubble wrap.

- Heavy felt for the base. The shape of the mat you create may be matched to your room space: pathlike, circular, or square.

What to Do

- Cut the heavy felt to the shape that will work for your space.

- Attach fabric and other materials securely to the mat base by gluing or sewing. Make sure that any sharp edges are covered. If you use a fabric bag filled with aquarium rock or other bumpy material, cover it twice to make sure it's safe for children.

- Place fabric and the other materials in room where infants will discover them on their own.

- Observe and reflect the children's reactions.

Limits

- You may have to help with traffic when more than one infant investigates the mat at the same time.

Other Things to Think About

- Consider making multiple mats with related materials, reversible mats, or mats that revolve around a certain theme, such as sound or texture.

Supporting Play

Use these strategies, shown in the following scenario, to support babies' investigation:

- Provide choices of materials and time to manipulate them.

- Offer information.

Midmorning in the infant room finds caregiver Lori on the floor with Susie, nine months old, and seven-month-old Steve. The texture mat is laid out in a twisty path. Susie comes across it as she crawls across the room. She crawls onto the mat, touching the piece of vinyl with her right hand. Susie pulls her hand back, shaking it like a cat touching water. "Oh, that piece is cold, isn't it," comments Lori. Susie reaches out to touch it, then shakes her head. "Go ahead, see how smooth it is," Lori encourages. Steve has rolled closer to see what is going on. He is on his tummy at one end of the mat and reaching toward a mound of fur. His right hand plops on top of it and rests. His left hand strokes the fur. "It's soft. The fur is very soft," Lori says. Susie has continued crawling on the mat. She stops, then starts crawling over the bumpy section. "That part is bumpy, Susie." "Bmmmm," says Susie.

Baby Hide-and-Seek

Infants are capable of understanding that an object still exists even though it is out of sight. But the ability to actually find a hidden object occurs around nine months. Caregiver and babies can have fun with this concept as caregiver observes play and presents opportunities for babies to look for a favorite object that is hidden.

What You'll Need

- Small toys like balls, rattles, or animal figures.
- Boxes, bowls, or scarves used to cover the toys.

What to Do

- Place small toys that can be hidden in the environment on the floor or a low shelf.
- Watch an infant play. Pay attention to a baby's reaction when a ball rolls under a shelf or out of sight. (Does she follow it with her eyes or go look for it?)
- Take the opportunity to hide a ball or other small toy underneath a bowl or a scarf, or in a box. Observe the baby's response.

Limits

None needed.

Other Things to Think About

- Other babies in the room may also want to play. Be prepared to hide small toys for each of them so they can make their own discoveries.
- If the babies aren't interested, try again in a couple of weeks. As with all development, the time at which children are interested in object permanence varies.

Supporting Play

Use these strategies, shown in the following scenario, to support children's play:

- Extend exploration.
- Promote self-awareness.

Ten-month-old Mary is doing a "G.I. Jane" crawl across the carpet. She stops and rolls from her side to a sitting position when she comes across a basket of key chain rattles, all having keys in them. Smiling, she picks one up and looks at caregiver Barbara. "I see you found the keys," she comments. Mary nods once and drops the first rattle for a different one. She shakes this one tentatively and drops it. The third key chain elicits a huge smile (the keys are hanging on a cow) and vigorous shaking. The keys go flying. Barbara says "Uh-oh, where did they go?" Mary looks surprised, and she crawls off in the opposite direction from where the cow key chain landed. Barbara gets the key chain and a scarf and meets her. "Here they are, Mary," Barbara says. When Mary looks and grunts "Eh, eh," Barbara covers them with the scarf. Mary raises her chest and wheels around to crawl over and whisk off the scarf. "You found the cow keys!" Barbara says as Mary shakes them, smiling and humming to herself.

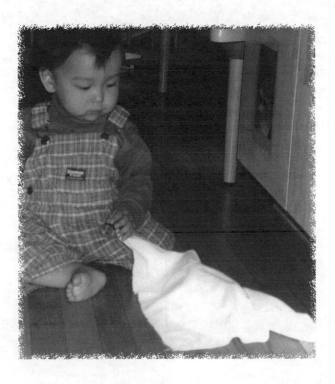

Making Music, Hearing Sounds

Sound makers or bells secured in the environment give infants the opportunity to make music or other sounds when they want to.

What You'll Need

- Large bells, hollow bamboo tube, sturdy tin or cardboard drum, or other sound-producing devices. These should be sturdy enough that children can bang on them with other materials from the environment, but they should also make noise if the children use only their hands to tap them.

What to Do

- Attach the sound makers securely to railings, walls, or shelves in the infant space.
- Observe the infants as they discover the noisemakers.

Limits

None needed.

Other Things to Think About

- Noisemakers could be themed—all bells, for instance, of different pitches.
- Plan to change noisemakers as babies lose interest.

Supporting Play

Use these strategies, shown in the following scenario, to support children's discovery of cause and effect:

- Plan to extend the exploration using children's interests as a guide.

> *Infant caregiver Kiana has seeded the infant area with bells. Big jingle bells securely sewn onto canvas straps are tied onto railings around the play area. One is placed low to the floor. Five-month-old Nasser rolls toward it, reaching with his right arm. He rolls onto to his back and tries again, this time rolling over and bumping the bells in the process. Kiana is on the floor near him and meets his gaze, smiling. Nasser scooches a bit and intentionally strikes the bells. "Oh, you made the bells jingle," Kiana says. Nine-month-old Rose is cruising along the railing. Looking at Nasser and back to the railing, she approaches the hanging bells. Grabbing them with both hands, she slides down to the floor and they jingle loudly. Quickly pulling up, she holds the railing with one hand and bats at the bells with the other. "The bells make a tinkly sound—I like them too," says Kiana. She brings out some hand bells, setting two close to each baby for further exploration.*

Family Boxes

Introducing images that may be unfamiliar to infants by connecting them first with familiar photos may enlist brain development in anti-bias work. Connections are made in the brain to identify "known" and "unknown." Caregivers can expand what is known by infants to develop self-concept, trust, and connection.

This idea came from a presentation by Valerie Rhomberg in 2000.

What You'll Need

- Boxes (like shoe boxes) with lids.
- Con-Tact paper in bold patterns and clear.
- Photos of the infants and their families, and photos of other families of a variety of cultures and ethnicities.

What to Do

- Cover the outside and lid of a box with patterned Con-Tact paper. (You may want to use more than one box.)
- After the infants have investigated the box for a time and the box itself is less interesting to them, add photos of them and their families to the outside of the box by attaching them with clear Con-Tact paper on top of the patterned paper.
- Again, after infants have had time to explore the box with the familiar photos on it, add similar images of other families from a variety of cultures and ethnicities (perhaps in the same family configuration).
- Then, when the newness wears off again, put something inside the box that is related to a photo on the outside of the box, for example, a hat, scarf, toy, or other item that appears in the photo.

Limits

- Boxes are not for chewing; provide teethers for chewing.

Other Things to Think About

- Human brains thrive on the "new." It is the new thing that sparks brain connections that lead to learning. In the context of the familiar, the unfamiliar may be understood.

Supporting Play

Use these strategies, shown in the following scenario, to support children's connections with others:

- Include family culture.
- Affirm mutual interests to encourage interdependence.

After a week of playing with three boxes covered in black-and-white check, red stripes, and green bull's-eye patterns, the babies are barely looking at them. Caregiver Lynn has added photos of the babies—eleven-month-old Maha, ten-month-old Laura, and eight-month-old Nick—and their families to the boxes. After lunch, Nick notices the different configuration on one of the box tops from three feet away, and he crawls over to investigate. It's a picture of Maha's family, and although he glances at Maha, it's hard for Laura to be sure he made the connection. She says, "That's a picture of Maha's family." When Nick comes across the box with his family on it, there is no doubt. "Dada, Ma. Dada, Ma," he repeats, holding the box close to his face. Maha is attracted to Nick's excitement and crawls over to see. Laura is there to guide her to the two unused boxes, affirming, "You both want to see the pictures," when Maha tries to take Nick's box. Maha quickly recognizes her family, pointing and saying "Der Tee, der Tee," when she sees her older brother's photo. Laura shares in the babies delight and makes plans to be sure they all are "introduced" to the other babies' pictures. Next week, she will add photos of other families that may be unfamiliar to these babies.

One Thing at a Time

When you are with one crawling baby for even a short time (for example, while other babies are asleep), offer the baby the opportunity to focus on one play object. This is also an opportunity for the caregiver to observe the child's individual approach and specific interests.

What You'll Need

- A single object or toy that the mobile infant has shown interest in, or a completely new object.

- Consider choosing specifically sense-related toys, such as a chime ball, a mirror ball, a soft toy, a hard box, or an unusual teether.

What to Do

- Clear the floor space and place one chosen object in the middle.

- When the infant enters the space—after eating or a diaper change, for example— observe her reaction.

Limits

None needed.

Other Things to Think About

- If two babies are present, try putting out two objects to see how they react to the toys and to each other.

- This is a wonderful opportunity for one-on-one time when other babies are sleeping.

- Doing this often with each baby allows a caregiver to observe each child's interests and the different ways the babies approach something new.

Supporting Play

Use these strategies, shown in the following scenario, to support children's play:

- Slow the pace ("Be an island").

> *Nine-month-old Amy is on the floor after eating her lunch. She rocks back on her bottom momentarily before rolling into a smooth crawl across the floor. She looks over to caregiver Vanessa once, who has placed a chime ball in the center of an otherwise clear floor. Amy heads directly for it, doggedly taking about ten crawling steps to get near it. She reaches out, takes one more step to touch it, and pushes the ball. Rocking back to a sit, Amy uses both hands to push at the ball, smiling at the sound it makes. "Oh!" says Vanessa, "You liked how the ball rolled when you pushed it. Did you hear the chimes?" Amy continues pushing, moving, and sliding the ball with her hand. She pauses when the ball chimes and tries another motion with her foot. Amy crawls after the chiming ball with a big smile on her face.*

Challenge Crawl

Infants who are crawling will welcome the challenge of shaped foam barriers attached to the carpet with Velcro.

What You'll Need

- Large pieces of foam to cover and make into pillows in a variety of shapes (cylinder, prism, cube, ramp).
- Heavy-duty hooked Velcro.

What to Do

- Make various shapes with the foam, about 12 to 18 inches high.
- Cover the shapes with fabric to make them durable and keep children from ripping or biting off pieces.
- Attach the hooked Velcro to one side of each shape. The shapes should then stick to the carpet.
- Put the shapes out on the rug so that babies discover them after nap or first thing upon arrival.
- Observe their reaction and respond with coaching.

Limits

None needed.

Other Things to Think About

- Make the pillows long enough for two babies at a time to negotiate them. This will facilitate parallel play.

- Double-sided sticky carpet tape could be used to secure pillows to the floor. Or you could drape a blanket over them to hold them in place.

Supporting Play

Use these strategies, shown in the following scenario, to foster infants' coordination practice:

- Promote body awareness by coaching.

- Facilitate problem solving with observation and open-ended questions.

While the babies were sleeping, caregiver Ling has set up two rows of shaped pillows that have been attached to the rug with Velcro. One is a prism shape, the other a rectangle. When nine-month-old Riley is ready for play, he finds them as he crawls across the room. Looking back over his shoulder at Ling, Riley grabs the peak of a pillow. Ling suggests, "Push with your feet," and Riley hoists himself over, grazing his chin as he lands. "Riley, I saw you climb that mountain," Ling comments. Riley easily hoists up onto the top of the rectangle. "Uh-oh, here's another one!" Ling says. "Try both hands," and Riley pauses before reaching down with both hands this time. "You made it," Ling says.

Find-and-Pull Toys

Tiny babies learn to pull on toys for a desired reaction. Older babies can use strings as tools.

What You'll Need

- Rolling toys with strings (a bead or ring on the end of the string for a handle is useful).

- Find-and-pull toy. To make your own:
  - A cardboard tube with a lid on one end, open on the other end.
  - A small toy that easily fits inside the tube.
  - A sturdy piece of string.
  - A large wooden bead or ring.

What to Do

- To make your own find-and-pull toy:
  1. Poke a hole in the tube's lid for the string.
  2. Put the lid on the tube.
  3. Pull a piece of string through the hole in the lid. Make the string a couple of inches longer than the tube.
  4. Attach the toy to the end of the string that comes out the open end of the tube. Attach a wooden bead or a ring for pulling to the other end. The toy should be hidden in the tube when the child pulls on the ring or bead.

- Line up three or four toys that have strings to pull. Babies who are comfortable on their tummies or rolling to the side can grasp the string to pull the toy to themselves.

- Include two or three find-and-pull toys in the environment.

Limits

- Make sure the strings are shorter than 12 inches so they won't get wrapped around a child's neck or tangled up around feet and in order to discourage swinging the heavier toy.

Other Things to Think About

- Observe each baby's interests, and the different way each approaches something new.

Supporting Play

Use these strategies, shown in the following scenario, to support children's skill integration:

- Make room for trial and error and repeated investigation.

Six-month-old Jock is lying on his tummy facing a line of strings. Caregiver Jada has placed four toys that have strings to pull them on the floor. Jock pulls a string with a red bead at the end, drawing the toy dog closer to himself. Then he pulls the next string in line—this one has a blue bead on the end. It's attached to the rolling toy bear. Jock looks back and forth between the toys. Jada says, "There's a bear and a dog." Jock starts to reach toward the next string, but switches and pulls the dog closer. "Oh, I see you like the dog," Jada says. Jock shoves the dog; it rolls away. While he's watching it closely, nine-month-old Simone is sitting with a find-and-pull tube toy. After pulling the string that hides the toy, she tries to reach inside to get it out. Her hand won't fit, and she holds the toy out toward Jada. "Yes, the lion is still inside. What else can you do?" Simone shakes it, but since she's holding onto the string, the toy doesn't fall down. "Try again," Jada suggests.

INFANTS

Water Pillow

Make a simple water pillow for babies to look at and push to cause items inside to move in the water.

What You'll Need

- Resealable bags in the largest size, at least two for each pillow.
- Duct tape to tightly close the water-filled bags.

What to Do

- Fill one bag about half full with water.
- Add small, bright, waterproof ornaments, figures, or shapes to the water.
- Close the bags, extracting as much air as possible.

You may experiment with the level of water—is it enough to cause "waves," but not too much? Do the figures move through the water?

- Seal the bags with duct tape.
- Enclose each water-filled bag inside another resealable bag, and tape the opening closed.
- Place in the babies' space.

Limits

- Bags are not for chewing; provide teethers.

Other Things to Think About

- If the water pillows will be exposed to toddlers, let the children know they must be gentle with them.

Supporting Play

Use these strategies, shown in the following scenario, to support children's interests:

- Plan to extend the exploration using child's interests as a guide.

When ten-month-old Zachi crawls across the room, he encounters a plastic bag filled with water and red and blue sponge shapes. Rocking back onto his bottom, he reaches out with his right hand. Slowly he draws one finger over the surface. "Mimi ha da," Zachi exclaims. "Oh, I see you found the water pillow," caregiver Susan says. "It's smooth." Zachi pats the surface with his right hand twice, then with both hands. The sponges bounce. Rolling over on his side, Zachi reaches with his foot to pat the pillow. Susan brings another water pillow filled with soap bubbles into the play space. Zachi crawls to it and lifts up one corner, looking back and forth between it and Susan. "See the bubbles?" she asks.

Baby Gym

Appropriate use of commercial baby gym frames can enhance infants' development from initial curiosity to coordination practice. It is possible to make use of a frame without trapping a nonmobile baby directly under it. Use of a baby gym can be consistent with respectful care by placing the infant next to the frame rather than underneath it. This can give the infant access to the hanging items with feet, hands, and mouth. The infant is able to reach and roll over to play with the dangling toys, as well as observing what else is happening in the room, if she wishes.

What You'll Need

- Sturdy frame with a wide variety of play options (for example, a frame with spinning, hanging, noise-making, and textured surfaces).

- Space to set aside the frame so that nonmobile babies are safe and not overrun by older infants.

What to Do

- Set up a sturdy frame so a noncrawling baby can be next to it, have room to roll toward and reach the hanging, spinning elements, and still be able to see around the room.

Limits

- Provide furniture for other children to pull up on, so they don't try to use the baby gym, which isn't meant for that purpose.

Other Things to Think About

- Babies of various ages will use the frame differently day to day and as they develop.

Supporting Play

Use these strategies, shown in the following scenario, to extend this experience:

- Provide a choice of materials and time to manipulate them.
- Provide opportunities to practice at varied levels of skill.
- Promote body awareness by coaching.

Four-month-old Maya arches her back and flails her arms. Today caregiver Tom lays her next to a baby gym, where she can reach the spinning toys mounted on the crossbar at the end. Her flailing arms intermittently hit the spinners. They move, and Maya stops for a moment before repeating the action. Arching her back repeatedly, she next bends her knees and rolls sideways toward the spinners. "Maya, I see you rolled onto your side. I can tell you want that toy bear under the gym," Tom says. In the future he plans to arrange toys Maya can kick at as she works on lifting her legs and "throwing" her weight in order to eventually turn over.

INFANTS

Step Right Up!

Take advantage of steps to set up an environment to be enticing to young crawlers and challenging for competent crawlers. Sturdy cardboard boxes or commercially made large carpet-covered blocks may be used.

What You'll Need

- Sturdy cardboard boxes stuffed with newspaper to make big blocks approximately 6 by 12 by 24 inches.

- Commercially made wooden blocks (open on one side and covered with carpet).

- Pillows, mats, or other padding to make the floor around the boxes safe for short tumbles.

What to Do

- Set up blocks in stair-step fashion. Make sure they are steady and not wiggly to provide a solid surface for babies to crawl on. They could lead to a window for infants to look out of, or they could go up one side and down the other.

- Place pillows or other padding where children might tumble down.

- Give infants your full attention, especially if they are negotiating steps for the first time.

Limits

- Older infants may attempt to stand on the steps. Help them remember where they are in space by being close and spotting them, using phrases like, "You're on the steps."

Other Things to Think About

■ Steps may be seeded with small toys to interest babies in climbing.

Supporting Play

Use these strategies, shown in the following scenario, to support children's play:

■ Provide for practice at varied levels of skill.

■ Promote body awareness by coaching.

> Caregiver Maggie has used nap time to set up steps leading to the window in the infant room. She adds a small stuffed animal on each level. After the babies awake and are settled in to play, ten-month-old Carmel is the first to crawl to the steps. Stopping at the bottom, she turns to look at Maggie, then points at the stairs. "I built stairs for you to get up and see out of the window. Go ahead, it's okay," Maggie tells her and moves closer to spot Carmel. Twelve-month-old Sam crawls by, heading directly up the stairs. "There's room for you on this side, Carmel," Maggie coaches. "You can go up too." Carmel kneels and puts her hands on the first step, puts one knee up, then the other. She's stuck on one step, so Maggie helps: "Can you figure it out? Move to the next step up here?" She pats the next step. Carmel freezes for ten seconds, and Maggie suggests, "Put your hand up here," and pats the next step again. Carmel takes another ten seconds to move her hand, then moves up the stairs slowly. Sam has pulled to a stand at the windowsill and is waving at the outdoors, "Bir, bir, tee!" Seven-month-old Shiri has just made it to the bottom of the stairs, moving like a seal—raise chest, pull with arms, and flop! At the stairs, she is able to pull up on the bottom step and gets her knees under her for the first time. She's content to lean on the step and play with a toy she finds there.

Infant Shape Sorter

Older infants extend their interest in metal lids through the problem-solving task of fitting the lids through slots and holes cut in the plastic tops of metal coffee cans.

What You'll Need

- Four clean coffee cans (approximately two-pound size) with plastic tops.
- Mat knife or other sharp edge to cut slits or circular holes in tops.
- Collection of clean smooth-edged metal juice lids (from frozen juice containers).

What to Do

- Cut rectangular slits in two of the plastic coffee can lids so that the metal juice can lids fit through upright. Cut circles in two other coffee can lids so that the juice can lids fit through as flat circles. Cut the circular hole slightly larger than a juice lid to ensure success.
- Let infants discover the cans in the environment; support their efforts toward getting the lids into the cans.

Limits

- Check the lids and cans periodically to see that they are smooth and rust-free. (They may rust after repeated washing.)

Other Things to Think About

- Be aware that many infants will require help in removing the plastic top to try again. Once the top is off, some will just put the lids directly into the can, delighting at the sound.

Supporting Play

Use these strategies, shown in the following scenario, to support children's play:

- Make room for trial and error and repeated investigation.
- Facilitate problem solving with observation and open-ended questions.

> *Ten-month-old Maddie clasps two metal lids in her hand as she sits with splayed legs on the floor. A can with a circular hole in the plastic top is to her right. At first, she bangs the juice lid onto the plastic top. Her next gesture is more precise—she pushes the metal lid around the plastic top to find the circular hole. Caregiver Rich notices her actions and says, "I see how you fit that lid into the can. There's another can with a different shaped hole in the lid. Can you figure that out too?" Maddie looks to her left and sees the other can with the slit-shaped hole. She repeatedly pokes the metal lid on the plastic top, then finds the slit. The metal lid clangs into the can. Maddie claps her hands.*

Fingerplays

Fingerplays can enhance connection between caregiver and infant as they engage together in routine experiences, such as diapering and dressing. They also provide a relaxing transition to play. The predictable manner in which these tasks are carried out builds trust between the caregiver and infant. These rhymes may be used as written or changed to reflect personal interests, arrival and departure, or cultural tradition.

What You'll Need

- A good repertoire of songs and fingerplays. (See below for a few suggested rhymes, and ask parents and other caregivers for more. You can also get books of fingerplays and rhymes at the library.)

What to Do

- At appropriate times—anticipating transitions, during dressing, or when babies engage you in play—respond by involving them in a rhyme related to a current happening or something that is visible or has been talked about.

Limits

None needed.

Other Things to Think About

- Older babies learn to anticipate what's coming next if the caregiver uses words like, "One more time and then we'll change your diaper."

- Ask parents to share their favorite or traditional rhymes and games.

Supporting Play

Use these strategies, shown in the following scenario, to involve children in routines and transitions:

- Be predictable and consistent in meeting children's needs.

- Slow the pace; be available ("Be an island").

Caregiver Linda has learned a number of fingerplay rhymes and uses them during routines when she cares for the infants. Audrey, Omar, and Miguel (six, nine, and ten months old, respectively) expect rhymes during routines. Omar claps his hands during diaper changes, and when it's complete they always do his favorite, "Clap Hands," supplying kisses and his name at the end. (See below.) Miguel joins in, clapping his hands from the shelf he's pulled up on. Audrey crawls over to Linda, who is sitting on the floor, and points at her own palm. Linda starts "Round and round the Garden," but Audrey pulls away. "Oh, you want 'This Little Cow?'" she asks. Nodding, Audrey returns.

Clap Hands

Clap hands, clap hands	*Clap hands in time to words.*
Til Daddy comes home	*Personalize with other caregiver's names and a variety of locations.*
He will bring goodies (hugs, kisses)	*Say baby's name.*
For baby alone.	

My Turtle

Here's my little turtle	*Make a fist and stick out your thumb.*
Here's her little shell.	*Hide your thumb in your fist.*
She likes her home very well.	
She pokes her head out,	*Extend your thumb.*
When she wants to eat,	
And pulls it back in,	*Hide your thumb again.*
When she wants to sleep.	

This Little Cow Eats Grass

This little cow eats grass,   *Hold baby's thumb.*
This little cow eats hay.   *Hold baby's forefinger.*
This little cow drinks water,   *Hold baby's middle finger.*
This little cow runs away.   *Hold baby's ring finger.*
This little cow does nothing,   *Hold baby's pinky finger.*
Except lie down all day.   *Tickle baby's pinky finger.*
We'll chase her, we'll chase her,   *Keep tickling all the way up the arm.*
We'll chase her away!

Cobbler, Cobbler Mend My Shoe

Cobbler, cobbler, mend my shoe.   *Knock fists together.*
Please be done by half past two,   *Shake your forefinger.*
Cause my toe is peeping through.   *Push your thumb through your fist and wiggle it.*
Cobbler, cobbler, mend my shoe.   *Knock fist together again.*

*From Baby's Games by Debby Slier © 1989 Checkerboard Press, Junior Elf Books Macmillan, Inc.
Used by permission.*

Con-Tact Paper Collage

Taping clear Con-Tact paper on a table top for young children to feel, stick other objects to and take them off engages them in exploring the concept of sticky.

What You'll Need

- Clear Con-Tact paper.

- Masking tape to adhere the Con-Tact paper to the table, sticky side up.

- Assorted materials and objects for children to stick on the Con-Tact paper, for example, shredded paper, feathers, Styrofoam packing peanuts, ribbon, and natural objects like leaves and seeds.

- Bowls or trays to contain the materials.

What to Do

- Tape one piece of Con-Tact paper to each side of a table with the sticky side up. Toddlers can sit or stand at the table.

- Fill small bowls with a variety of materials and place them in the middle of the table. (Younger toddlers may want their own tray or bowl with materials in it.)

- Invite a group of no more than four older infants or toddlers to "Come see what we have today."

- Allow the children to discover the sticky paper: "What does it feel like? What can you do?"

- They will put items onto the Con-Tact paper and take them off.

- Each group collage can be mounted low on a wall and be a continuing experience for a few days.

Limits

- Materials are for sticking on the Con-Tact paper and taking off, not for throwing.
- Provide soft alternatives for throwing.

Other Things to Think About

- Another time, toddlers might enjoy having their own square of Con-Tact paper. After a child is done placing materials on the Con-Tact paper (and taking them off), you can preserve the collage by putting a piece of construction paper of the same size on top so it adheres to the Con-Tact paper. You may need to tape around the edges to hold it together.

Supporting Play

Use these strategies, shown in the following scenario, to support children's play:

- Make room for trial and error and repeated investigation.
- Allow for innovative use of materials.

Fifteen-month-old Nolan takes the bowl in both hands and dumps out its contents. Thirty-three-month-old Martina says, "Pink, pink, stuck, it's stuck," as she works on one packing peanut at a time, smashing it to the clear Con-Tact paper. She takes some of the pieces off. Twenty-seven-month-old Donna is standing by the table. She extends her two index fingers, alternating them as she gently pokes a packing peanut on the paper. "It's bouncing," she comments. She repeats, using first two and then three fingers with similar results. Then she runs her hands underneath the Con-Tact paper, causing a ripple effect, but not dislodging the peanuts. Twenty-three-month-old Delino looks up from his book, drops it, and comes to the table. Martina gives him a feather, and Delino says thank you. He carefully takes out all the materials in his bowl, stacking them up in a pile on the paper. "More, please," he asks. Martina collects some materials in her bowl, then gives it to Delino, offering, "More?" and Delino says thank you. Two-year-old Aman approaches the table and asks, "Touch it?" Gina says, "Yes, touch it and see what you think." He pulls his hand away quickly when it sticks. Then he straightens a piece of shredded paper, "Broken," he says, placing it on the Con-Tact paper. Twenty-nine-month-old Al moves between the Lego table and the Con-Tact paper. He places some construction paper on the Con-Tact paper, then goes to the Lego table and returns with a Lego block. He sticks it on, then pulls it off.

What Are You Wearing Today?

Young babies spend much of their time near the caregiver, both during routines and while being held. Caregivers can choose clothing and accessories to enhance this time together. Toddlers also assimilate knowledge from keen observation of what a caregiver is wearing.

What You'll Need

- Comfortable clothes in a variety of patterns and textures.

- Other accessories, such as interesting jewelry (as long as it doesn't have small parts that can easily be detached by babies) or barrettes for long hair. Since babies are on the floor, even your socks can be the basis for engaging!

What to Do

- Notice the infants' reaction to what you are wearing. Does Dan like the red turtleneck? Does Susie snuggle more when you wear the pink fuzzy sweater that resembles her blanket?

- Comment on what you are wearing and children's responses. Use phrases like, "Oh, you like this bright yellow sweatshirt, don't you?"

- Respond to toddlers who make connections, for example, bringing you the stuffed panda when you wear a shirt with pandas on it.

Limits

None needed.

Other Things to Think About

- Be aware that this experience is meant as a response to what a child notices, rather than entertainment.

Supporting Play

Use these strategies, shown in the following scenario, to support children's interest in the people in their environment:

- Share the caregiver's interests ("Say who you are").

> *Caregiver Barb loves animals. Whenever she wears the shirt embroidered with wild animals, she knows twenty-month-old Beng will want lap time. Today he runs across the yard when she arrives, shouting "Zeba, zeba," before reaching her. They sit down together, and he points and names all the animals. "Monkey?" "Oh, this shirt doesn't have any monkeys," Barb tells him, making a mental note to wear the shirt that has monkeys on it tomorrow. Beng climbs off her lap to walk around her, patting the back of her shirt to make sure there are no monkeys.*

"Clean" Fingerpainting

New experiences can be created by combining unlikely materials. Discarded pages from "magnetic" photo albums act as an unusual canvas for fingerpainting. This is a nice way to extend fingerpainting for those children who are drawn to it, and it is a good way to interest those who don't like to get their hands messy.

Thanks to Jill Craddock for originating this experience.

What You'll Need

- "Magnetic" photo album pages. These are the ones that are made of heavy white cardboard or tagboard with a plastic cover held on by static electricity.

- Fingerpaint (washable) in three to five colors.

- Plastic spoons or Popsicle sticks to convey paint from jar to page.

- Smocks or oversized T-shirts, if desired.

- Wet and dry towels for cleanup.

What to Do

- Gather a group of no more than four older infants or toddlers.

- Help children into smocks.

- Explain that this will be a different way of fingerpainting and that all children will get a turn.

- Lift the clear plastic cover from an album page.

- Place a dime-sized dab of each color of paint on the page (use a Popsicle stick or plastic spoon).

- Children can choose what colors they want and help with the paint.

- Lay the clear plastic lightly over the paint; the child can help.

- Encourage the child to "paint" by pressing on the plastic to move the paint around underneath it.

Limits

▪ Materials stay on the table.

Other Things to Think About

▪ Consider using foam paint.

Supporting Play

Use these strategies, shown in the following scenario, to support children's play:

▪ Validate children's experience ("Say what you see").

▪ Provide choices of materials and time to manipulate them.

Caregiver Jill has gathered four toddlers to try a new experience. She knows that eighteen-month-old Heather has been reluctant to fingerpaint in the past. Today she will offer the protection of the plastic cover on the "magnetic" photo pages. Heather is sitting in front of a photo page with the blue and yellow paint she chose. Tentatively, she pokes at the cover; it gives a little, and the yellow paint squishes. Heather quickly slides the heel of her hand across the page and says, "Oooh." Jill says, "Oh, I see you spread the yellow paint across the page." Twenty-six-month-old Justin carefully pushes paint toward the middle of his page, using both hands. Slowly the red and blue come together. "Purple!" he says. "I see you mixed the red and blue," Jill comments. Two-year-old Nischal is very busy sliding both hands over the plastic. The paint squeezes along underneath. He lifts the plastic cover and says, "Look, it's two pictures!" "Oh, there is a picture on both sides," Jill says. Thirty-month-old Cara has smoothed her page and is using her finger to make little zigzags. "My name," she says. "You are writing your name?" Jill reflects. Cara lifts her plastic sheet and asks "Where's my name?" "Where do you think?" Jill asks. Cara puts down the plastic to look.

Cellophane Gluing and Viewing

Older infants and toddlers are fascinated by colored, lightweight, crinkly cellophane. A caregiver using it for gluing projects often finds toddlers spontaneously holding it up to look through it—follow their lead!

What You'll Need

- Cellophane in various colors.

- Bowls of glue with brushes.

- Tape.

- Paper to glue or tape cellophane onto (white intensifies the colors).

- Bowls, baskets, or trays to hold cellophane pieces.

What to Do

- Cut colored cellophane into small pieces for gluing. Place the pieces in a container for each toddler.

- Cut some pieces about 3 by 6 inches so that toddlers can hold them up in front of their eyes.

- Have glue bottles or dishes of glue with brushes ready for each toddler.

- Invite a small group of toddlers to investigate the materials.

- Reflect their comments and actions: "Oh, you're looking through the paper." "You have covered the whole paper with cellophane. Do you want to glue it on?" "It makes noise when you ball it up." "Oh, it fell off the paper. Do you want it to stay there? Let's try taping it."

Limits

- Decide ahead of time if it's acceptable or not for toddlers to ball up the cellophane and throw it. This is relatively safe, but it may use a lot of cellophane. Caregivers could limit the amount of cellophane used in this way.

- If cellophane is not for throwing, provide soft balls or socks as an alternative.

Other Things to Think About

- Prepare enough cellophane pieces or have the cellophane ready to cut so toddlers don't have to wait for more.

- Use cellophane in basic colors (red, blue, and yellow), and comment about mixed colors only if the toddlers express recognition of this.

Supporting Play

Use these strategies, shown in the following scenario, to support children's play:

- Validate the child's experience.

- Plan to extend the exploration using child's interest as guide.

- Offer information ("Say what you know").

Caregiver Eduardo invites four young children into the art room for an experience with colored cellophane. After they are around the table, he offers a tray with larger pieces of cellophane (3 by 6 inches) and they each choose some. Immediately, twenty-eight-month-old Derek says, "I like it," as he holds up a piece of cellophane in front of his eyes with both hands. "Can see you, can see you—yellow!" says Derek, moving his head and keeping the cellophane in front of his eyes. "What do you think?" Eduardo asks. "Going to turn off the light!" Derek answers, and switches from yellow to blue cellophane. Thirteen-month-old Hideo sits at the table, raising and lowering a piece of cellophane. "Der dum," he says, smiling. Two-year-old Lauren says hi to Hideo as she approaches. She holds up a red piece in front of his eyes. He looks through it. "Peekaboo!" she says, and he laughs. Twenty-nine-month-old Bret holds a red piece of cellophane over his eyes and looks at the ceiling light. "Paint that flashlight!" he says. Eduardo comments, "It's like painting the light, making it a different color. You remember when we experimented with flashlights." This experimentation goes on for three to five minutes before Derek says, "I need tape." Eduardo responds by sticking small lengths of tape (1 to 3 inches each) on the edge of the table by each child. He offers more colored pieces of cellophane in individual bowls for the children to tape onto the paper. Hideo continues looking through the cellophane, holding it up and pulling it away quickly.

Weighted Fleece

Curved fleece pillows filled with aquarium rock offer an open-ended prop for play and experimentation. They are interesting to a child's senses, being soft, bumpy, and heavy.

We first came across this idea in Transition Magician 2 *by Mary Henthorne, Nola Larson, and Ruth Chvojicek. St Paul: Redleaf Press, 2000.*

What You'll Need

- Fleece or fake fur fabric.

- Aquarium rock (use this because it's washable).

- Muslin fabric to make an inner bag to hold the rock.

- A pattern for a curved pillow about 4 inches wide by 12 to 15 inches long. A toddler-sized T-shirt is a good guide to making the pattern—make it big enough to go over both shoulders and around the neck hole.

What to Do

- To make the weighted pillows:
  1. Cut out matching pieces from both the fur and the muslin.
  2. Sew around the outer curve and around the ends of the lining.
  3. Sew in from the outer curve to within an inch of the inside curve three times to make four pockets spaced evenly to hold the aquarium rock.
  4. Fill to the point that you can still sew the curve closed (fat, but not bursting).
  5. Sew around the outer curve of the fur, right sides together.
  6. Turn right side out and fit the rock-filled lining inside the fur.
  7. Sew the fur closed (zigzag stitch works well).

- Seed the environment with four of these weighted fleeces.

- Allow the children to discover them, perhaps in the housekeeping corner or near a quiet pillow area.

- Respond to the children's questions and note their creative responses.

Limits

- The weighted fleeces are for carrying or wearing, not for swinging or throwing. Their weight makes them difficult to throw, and the curve discourages swinging.

Other Things to Think About

- Suggest the weighted fleeces to toddlers who are at loose ends or who have chosen to take a break but seem unable to settle in and relax.

- These can also be heated for 1 to 2 minutes in a microwave or clothes dryer. The heat is soothing and relaxing. They will stay warm for a long time.

Supporting Play

Use these strategies, shown in the following scenario, to support children's play:

- Promote self-awareness.

- Share your own interests ("Say who you are").

Rasheed discovers the weighted fleeces on the floor by the books. He lifts one and drapes it over his arm, then picks up two more. He is clutching them to his chest as he strides across the room. Caregiver Scott says, "I see you found the weighted pillows." Rasheed sits down, draping the pillows over his legs. "Worms," he says. "They are like worms, aren't they?" reflects Scott. "They are very big, though, and heavy. Do you like the way they feel?" Rasheed squirms under the fleeces. Meanwhile, Betty, also two years old, finds the other fleece. She picks it up and puts it directly around her neck. "Heavy," she says, walking a few steps before taking it off. Scott picks it up when she drops it. "It is heavy, isn't it. I kind of like the way it feels on my shoulders," he says.

Big Fabric Pieces

Using large pieces of fabric to make tents, awnings, lean-tos or other definitions of space can spark toddlers' imaginations and shade an infant from the sun.

This experience was originated by Jill Craddock.

What You'll Need

- Large pieces of fabric (6 by 6 feet or longer).
- Clips, cords, clothespins, tape, or other fastening devices.

What to Do

- Decide where to drape the fabric to create a tent, awning, or lean-to, and find places to attach the fabric. (You may want to do this when children are not around if it involves climbing on objects you don't want them to climb on.)
- One easy way to drape fabric is to throw it over two ropes (like a tent) so it forms two "walls" and a "ceiling."
- If there are structures or trees in the yard, it may be possible to secure a "canopy" between them by tying rope securely around the corners of the fabric and then to the trees or posts of structures to stretch the fabric in between. Also, there are do-it-yourself grommet kits to make secure eyelets to run rope through.
- Indoors, fabric can be secured to walls, woodwork, or climbing structures with duct tape, or with cup hooks if they will be out of children's reach.
- Clothespins or tape may be used to roll up and secure trailing edges of the fabric to lessen the attraction of pulling the structure down.

Limits

- Children should not pull on or hang from the material. Use phrases like these to help them find other ways of experimenting with it: "The material is not for pulling or hanging from." "Try sitting under it or inside." "How does it look?" "How does it feel?"

Other Things to Think About

- Provide an alternative to hanging on the fabric—for example, other pieces of fabric to carry around (larger than usual doll-blanket size). This will give children a new experience and the satisfaction of manipulating a large cloth. ("Streamers," page 243, or "Swinging on a Knotted Rope," page 219, both in *Infant and Toddler Experiences,* also might meet this need.)

- Try setting up two real tents in the yard. Having two gives a choice of space to toddlers and minimizes conflict.

Supporting Play

Use these strategies, shown in the following scenario, to support children's play:

- Offer information ("Say what you know").

- Share your interests ("Say who you are"), and acknowledge the children's response.

Jill draped a large piece of fabric on top of the A-frame structure. Thirty-four-month-old Otis says, "It's a new house!" "Yes," said Jill, "we remodeled." She continues setting up the yard by hanging a large piece of fabric over some low branches of trees and putting a rug on the ground underneath. Placing some dolls and blankets inside, she waits for toddlers to discover the area. "Babies," says eighteen-month-old Yarden. "The babies are under the canopy," Jill reflects. Thirty-three-month-old Kalena says "Tent! Tent!" as she runs outdoors. "It does look like a tent, doesn't it? Do you remember sleeping inside a tent when we went camping?" Jill asks.

Photo Albums and Pages

Infants and toddlers recognize themselves, their friends, and their caregivers in photographs. They especially enjoy laminated pages that are easy to hold, carry around, and look at with others.

What You'll Need

- Photographs of people in the center's community: children, caregivers, custodians, cooks, families.

- Laminator or clear Con-Tact paper or commercial vinyl page protectors.

- Heavy paper or thin cardboard for mounting photos; approximately 8½ by 11 inches.

- Tape or gluestick to hold the photos in place when laminating or covering with clear Con-Tact paper.

- Poster-sized paper, 24 by 36 inches.

What to Do

- Place at least a dozen 8½-by-11-inch photo pages in the environment for infants and toddlers to discover on their own.

- Connect people's names to their photo *and* their relationship to the children.

- Respond to questions ("Who's that?" "That is Erin's mom, Heidi"), comments, and excitement at finding their own photos.

- Reflect questions back: "Who does it look like?" "What do you think?"

- Facilitate looking at the pages together, trading, and taking turns.

Limits

- Promote respect. Use phrases like "be gentle," and "not for chewing." Provide alternatives, such as teethers, to meet the need to chew.

- Encourage peers to look at photos together and talk about what they see ("Can you tell what's happening?").

Other Things to Think About

- Photos may be mounted by theme or season. (See "Photo Album" in *Infant and Toddler Experiences*, page 172.)

- Mount photos of toddlers taken when they were babies and see who they can recognize.

- Put photos on poster-sized tagboard and hang at child-height.

- Show the children photos of caregivers when they were infants and toddlers.

Supporting Play

Use these strategies, shown in the following scenario, to encourage children's interest in recognizing others:

- Introduce peers and adults by name.

- Affirm mutual interests to encourage interdependence.

Twenty-eight-month-old Joel says, "Look, look!" Caregiver Roberto responds, "I see the picture of you." Joel nods slowly. "Of a little boy," Joel says. "Yes, those pictures were taken last summer. Remember playing in the water? You were littler then." Others are looking at pages of photos taken at the recent camp-out and of indoor and outdoor experiences at the center. Twenty-seven-month-old Adriana squeals in delight, pointing at the photo of Rachelle, who is a special friend. Two-year-old Ellis recognizes photos of the babies. "Der's Ari," he points out, even though Ari is older and walking now. Fourteen-month-old Roberto sits on a pillow, carefully turning the page over and back, saying, "Doodle doodle." Sixteen-month-old Tricia points precisely at one photo at a time, identifying "Tee, house, pip, Leni, Fran." Fran repeats after her, "Tree, house, Phillip, Eleni, Fran—I see you know everyone in all those pictures!"

Velcro Lids

Connections are made as children look at pictures of themselves, peers, or familiar objects on metal juice lids. The lids can be carried around or placed on and off a Velcro backing. (The backing may be mounted on the back of a toy shelf or another vertical surface.)

Thanks to Maryann Keisselbach for originating this experience.

What You'll Need

- Clean lids, without sharp edges or points. Metal lids from frozen juice cans work well.

- Con-Tact paper.

- Photos or pictures from magazines of familiar people and objects, small enough to fit on a lid.

- Velcro with sticky backing.

- Large piece of the loop side of Velcro mounted on a vertical surface, such as the back of a toy shelf. Some toy shelves come equipped with this backing.

What to Do

- Cut out photos to fit onto the lids and use Con-Tact paper to attach each photo to the side of the lid that has a lip around it.

- Place a small piece of the hook side of Velcro (½-inch square) onto the flat side of the lid.

- Have a lot of lids for toddlers to collect, sort, and carry around (thirty to forty for four children).

- Place the lids in containers and seed the environment with them, or simply stick them on the Velcro backing and let the children discover them.

- Be available to observe and facilitate trading and taking turns.

Limits

- Lids are not for chewing on or throwing.

- Provide alternatives for these actions, such as teethers and soft balls or balled-up socks. (See "Soft Objects to Throw Indoors" in *Infant and Toddler Experiences*, page 234.)

- Support innovative ideas; for example, use the lids in play centered around cooking near the housekeeping area.

Other Things to Think About

- Velcro may also stick to carpeting.

- You might want to produce specific sets of lids for organized play: food, toys, familiar and unfamiliar faces, animals, vehicles, people in uniform or work clothes, or categories of objects (hats, shoes, buildings).

Supporting Play

Use these strategies, shown in the following scenario, to support children's play:

- Affirm mutual interests to encourage interdependence.

- Encourage taking turns and trading.

There are two dozen lids stuck with Velcro onto the back of a cabinet in the housekeeping area. More lids are stored in a bag hanging on the end of the shelf. Most of these lids have food or animal pictures. Fourteen-month-old Pat walks to the display and reaches for one. She pulls it off, using both hands. "I did it," she says, and turns to stick it back on. It sticks, and she says, "I did it again," looking toward caregiver Mike. He says, "Pat, I see you taking those lids off and putting them back on." Nodding, Pat pulls off more, collecting three and walking to the table. Twenty-seven-month-old Roger swoops behind her, taking off eight of the lids. Moving to an open space, he lines them up on the floor. The Velcro sticks to the carpeting. When Roger tries to move them, he discovers that he can't and appeals to Mike, saying, "Stuck, stuck." Mike suggests that he can pull them off just as he pulled them off the shelf. "Here, here, a carrot," says Roger. "Yes, I see the carrot. There are some other vegetables too, " Mike comments. Roger takes the lid with a carrot picture on it into the housekeeping area and puts it in a pan. Twenty-two-month-old Nat comes by and picks up a lid from the rug. "A penny," she says. "A penny?" Mike says. "Yup, a penny and a sticker!" Nat says with obvious delight. Pat comes to see this wonderful penny and tries to grab it. Mike reminds her that she has lids on the table. "Why don't you see if Nat will trade lids with you?" he suggests, guiding her back to her collection.

Hanging Sounds

Bells, pots, pans, and lids hang from a fence or room divider with cardboard tubes for children to make sounds.

What You'll Need

- Metal containers in a variety of weights: aluminum bowls, steel pans, cast iron pots and lids.
- Curved S-hooks, duct tape, or rope.
- Cardboard tubes for strikers.

What to Do

- Hang pans and lids on a fence at intervals that will enable more than one child to play with them but close enough together for a single child to compare the differing sounds. Use S-hooks, duct tape, or string or rope, depending on the fence.
- Hang a cardboard striker by each pan or lid.
- Watch and wait, allowing children to discover the pans and lids on their own.
- Reflect children's response and experimentation.

Limits

- Strikers are for pans and lids only. Offer alternatives for hitting (see "Hanging Balls Outdoors," page 161). Help children take turns and trade.

Other Things to Think About

- Consider hanging a variety of objects from the fence: large bells, wide pieces of bamboo, or wooden bowls.
- You can also use a board to hang the music makers. Drill holes in the board to insert S-hooks or rope, and attach the board securely to the fence.
- Protect the music makers from the weather, if necessary.

Supporting Play

Use these strategies, shown in the following scenario, to support children's interdependence and their learning how to resolve conflict:

- For every no, give two yeses.
- Affirm mutual interests to encourage interdependence.

Caregiver Bill has hung a stainless steel mixing bowl, a cookie tin, and a skillet from the fence. There are paper towel tubes nearby. When the toddlers come outdoors, a few come to see the new toys. Bill is nearby as fourteen-month-old Ian lifts the cookie tin and lets it crash against the metal mesh fence. The sound is loud, but musical and high-pitched. Ian says, "Uh-oh," and picks it up to drop it again. "It makes a sound when you drop it against the fence," Bill says. Twenty-month-old Claire comes to investigate. She takes the tin from Ian. Ian screams, " Mine!" Bill says, "You both want to make the sounds, but Ian is using the cookie tin now." Then he turns to Claire and says, "I can't let you take the tin from Ian. You can bang on the skillet or wait your turn." Claire pats the skillet with her right hand before lightly banging the skillet with the cardboard. Moving over to the bowl, she gets a more satisfactory ringing. "Sing, sing," she says. "It does sound like the bowl is singing," Bill answers.

Mirroring

Caregivers find themselves mirroring or imitating infants' facial expressions as a matter of course. Extending this mirroring to body gestures and verbal utterances connects caregivers and all ages of children over time, leading to an interactive game. Toddlers love to be the leader as caregivers mirror their movements, sounds, and actions. This reciprocal interaction between caregiver and child models a conversation.

What You'll Need

No materials needed for this experience.

What to Do

- Begin by mirroring an infant's facial expressions, sounds, or rhythms as they exhibit them, then engage the child by making eye contact. For example, respond to clapping by clapping your hands; blinking, waving, in the same manner.

- Older toddlers may ask what you are doing, and you can explain, then ask them, "Would you like to try it?"

- The caregiver and child can take turns being the leader and follower.

Limits

- If toddlers try to mirror each other, think ahead about ground rules. For example, say, "Use your eyes to watch, then mirror or do what you see him do." An exception to this rule may be made when the interaction comes to an end and a hug could be offered to say, "That was fun to do with you."

Other Things to Think About

- Be mindful of including all the senses when you are the leader.

Supporting Play

Use these strategies, shown in the following scenario, to support infants' and toddlers' trust and autonomy:

- Honor verbal and nonverbal communication.

- Be predictable and consistent in meeting children's needs.

- Slow the pace; be available (Be an "island").

When six-month-old Freddie came to the center, he was unhappy for long stretches during the day. In a happy moment, he made a trilling sound with his tongue against the roof of his mouth. Caregiver Judy made the trilling sound right back. Freddie broke into a big smile, then repeated the sound. Judy trilled right back. Scooching over to where she was sitting on the floor, he climbed into her lap to continue the trilling conversation.

Juanita, fifteen months old, and two-year-old Bruce are visiting in the baby room. They approach Freddie and Judy. Bruce says, "What donin?" Judy explains that she is following Freddie's actions. "Let me show you," she says, "I'll do what you do." When Bruce tips his head, she does the same. When he shakes it, she shakes hers. "Now you try it," Judy suggests. And she waves her hand. "You're waving your hand like I am." After two turns, Judy sees that Bruce would rather be the leader, so she trades roles with him.

Introduce Cultural Variations of Home Life

Infants and toddlers are first tuned in to their own family culture. Here are a few examples of introducing multicultural experiences that are meaningful to infants and toddlers. By including a variety of implements, toys, clothes, and books, care-givers can help all the children see their family culture reflected in the program. All the children then have opportunities to make connections between the familiar and the unfamiliar.

What You'll Need

- Many of the following items could be introduced in the housekeeping or family life corner. Be sure to begin with items that are used by the children's families. Ask them what tools would be appropriate to bring into the housekeeping area.

  Asian soup spoons

  Asian rice paddles

  Asian steamer baskets

  A variety of shaped cups, decorated plates and dishes in wood, metal, and plastic

  Dress-up clothes including vests, aprons, quilted jackets, and clothes made in traditional fabrics

  A variety of clothes for different climates: hats, gloves, boots, shoes, socks, sun suits

- Many of the following items could be introduced outdoors as toys for large-muscle play.

  football

  soccer ball

  volleyball

  basketball

  shovel-shaped baskets similar to jai alai baskets

  sticks and hoops

What to Do

- Add cultural items to different areas a few at a time, remembering to duplicate items to avoid conflicts.

- Begin with items that are familiar to one or more of the children in your program and items that have analogs in the cultural lives of most of the children (for example, different kinds of pots, bowls, shoes, or spoons).

Limits

- Guide the children to use items appropriately by giving two yeses for every no. Provide alternatives for throwing and hitting.

Other Things to Think About

- When setting up the environment, include examples from the children's homes. Ask them what utensils, dishes, clothes, toys, or sports equipment they use, even if it's only for special cultural celebrations. Parents are wonderful resources for the kinds of items they use and what they do in their own homes. For example, in Silicon Valley, computer keyboards and cell phones are cultural toys. In another culture, fabric in a small embroidery hoop might be more familiar to the children.

- Display writing from other countries. In our experience, families have brought us toys from Europe and the Middle East. We keep the boxes the toys came in showing the different languages for the children to see whenever we use them.

- Display grocery bags with a variety of languages printed on them.

- Use newspapers with a variety of languages to cover the tables or floors for painting and other projects.

Supporting Play

After thoughtfully setting up the environment, use these strategies (shown in the following scenario) to encourage children's connections with themselves and others.

- Include family culture.

- Affirm mutual interests to encourage interdependence.

Yukiko and Ken, both two-and-a-half years old, are playing in the housekeeping area. Caregiver Jen hears them talking about how they are making dinner. She is close by. Soon Yukiko brings her a bowl and a spoon. "Here's your dinner." "Thank you. What am I eating?" Jen asks. "Soup first," Yukiko answers and returns to the kitchen. Twenty-two-month-old Leah comes to Jen. "Whatsit?" she asks. "This is a soup spoon," Jen answers. "Spoo," Leah says. Ken brings a steamer, saying "Rice," and rushes back to the kitchen where Yukiko is trying to give him a plate. Jen makes a mental note to read Everybody Cooks Rice *with the children soon.*

Playdough

Playdough is such a common medium, planning may not seem necessary. However, it is good to review the opportunities this experience affords for caregivers to use strategies that support developing coordination. The tactile nature of the soft dough is therapeutic. Over time, caregivers will see children's increasing imagination and manual dexterity. This is suitable for very young children who are more interested in the tactile experience than in putting the playdough in their mouths.

What You'll Need

- Ingredients for playdough recipe (see below).

- Implements such as small cups, rollers, plastic picnic knives, plastic pizza cutters, melon ballers, or spoons. Having duplicates is more important than having variety.

What to Do

- Make playdough. A recipe with about 3 cups of flour produces enough for four to five toddlers.

  Playdough Recipe
  3 cups water
  3 cups white flour
  2 tablespoons cream of tarter
  ⅓ cup vegetable oil
  1½ cups salt

  Bring water and oil to a boil. Mix the flour and cream of tartar in a bowl. Then, on lowered heat, stir the salt into the water and oil until it dissolves. Next gradually add the flour and cream of tartar mixture. It may be lumpy at first, but it will become smooth as you stir. It will become very thick and pull away from the sides of the pan. Stir it as long as you can, then turn it out onto a floured tray or board and knead until it's completely smooth and elastic. Toddlers love the warmth—they can help knead it. (Soak the pan for easy cleanup later.) If you want colored playdough, add a few drops of food coloring to the water. Cake decorating color makes rich, intense colors of playdough. You can also make black and brown playdough using these colorings.

- Set out playdough and implements on a table. You may choose to give each child a small assortment of implements and her own hunk of playdough, or place one bowl of implements in the center of the table.

- Gather four children who are interested in playing with playdough.

- Allow the children their own experiences (poking, rolling, squeezing) while you reflect their actions.

Limits

- Playdough is for use at the table.

- Playdough is not for throwing or eating. Offer alternatives: soft things to throw or a teether to chew on.

- Encourage "pretend eating": Hold the playdough an inch from your mouth and make smacking sounds.

Other Things to Think About

- It is more helpful to model a technique than to manipulate the playdough for the children ("Try rolling it between your hands," instead of "This is how to make a worm"). Decide ahead of time how you will handle the difference between coaching and directing. It may be helpful to have a small piece of your own, both to model not destroying others' creations and to resist the temptation of making creations for the children or improving on theirs.

- Provide support for play as it emerges from the children. For example, for play that involves cooking the playdough, a part of the table or a small table close by might be a designated oven for baking.

- Plan experience times that do not include any implements so the children experience just the feeling of the playdough in their hands.

Supporting Play

There are many ways to support children's play using this most open-ended of materials. In the following scenario, the caregiver used these strategies:

- Provide opportunities for practice at varied levels of skill.

- Facilitate problem solving with observation and open-ended questions.

- Promote body awareness by coaching ("Try rolling it," "Use two hands," "Tell me what it is exactly you want to do," "Keep trying different ways").

A conversation is taking place around a table where four toddlers are engrossed in a new batch of playdough. Phillip says, "I'm making a flower." Flattening the playdough between his hands, he says, "Tight, tight, tight." He says to himself, "This, this, this sticky." Caregiver Jeff sits with the children, supplying extra flour for the sticky dough and reflecting the action: "You're making a flower?" Typically, the toddlers talk around each other. Jim says, "I'm cutting a piece. I'm making apple seeds for Johnny Appleseed. I'm Johnny Appleseed." Jeff says, "Oh, what are you going to do?" Jim answers, "He makes apple seeds." Phillip says, "I made a nana." Jeff asks, "A banana?" Phillip says, "Yes!" Keishi sticks her thumb in her ball of dough and lifts the whole thing up off the table, grins, and lets it fall. Allison says, "Look, like this," and squashes and kneads her ball of dough. Ari cuts a small piece off with a pizza cutter and rolls it expertly to make a worm. Soon everybody is making worms or snakes. Jeff models the technique of holding one's hand flat and rolling it "back and forth and back and forth."

Balancing Practice

Infants and toddlers will make anything into a hat. Toddlers who have mastered walking might enjoy the challenge of walking while balancing blocks on their heads. This experience can be adapted for indoors or outdoors.

What You'll Need

- Lightweight blocks, such as hollow cardboard blocks, or small wooden cubes.
- Other balancing materials, such as small bowls, scarves, or baskets.

What to Do

- Invite a small group of toddlers to practice balancing blocks on their heads.
- Model balancing the block on your head.
- The children will be eager to try. Help them place the blocks on their heads, and be encouraging if they fall.
- Offer easier materials, such as bowls, scarves, or baskets, if they grasp the idea but are having difficulty balancing the blocks.

Limits

- These blocks are for balancing practice. There are other blocks for building.
- Blocks are not for throwing. Have soft objects available as alternatives.

Other Things to Think About

- Consider having toddlers practice in front of a mirror.

Supporting Play

Use these strategies, shown in the following scenario, to help children learn to solve problems.

- Promote body awareness by coaching.

> *"Danny, I see you have a basket on your head," caregiver Ed comments. He is out in the yard. Soon more children are parading around with baskets on their heads. Using a lightweight cardboard block, Ed models balancing it on his head. Twenty-seven-month-old Danny drops his basket and comes to get a block. "Stand still to balance the block before you try to walk," Ed suggests. When it keeps sliding off after three tries, Ed asks a group to go indoors, where there are small wooden blocks. Danny more easily balances a 3-inch wooden block while walking. Twenty-two-month-old Lettie tries, and Ed suggests she stand in front of the mirror. "See what happens when you move your head?" he asks. Nineteen-month-old Nancy picks up the block that falls from her head as if to throw it. Ed offers a soft ball and a scarf: "You could throw this ball or try walking with the scarf on your head."*

Markers

This most basic art experience gives infants and toddlers the opportunity to express themselves in color. The lightest touch produces a mark.

What You'll Need

- Washable markers, at least one set for each child.

- Paper in a variety of colors, sizes, and textures.

- Baskets or bowls to hold markers for each child.

What to Do

- Choose materials ahead of time. Decide on a particular paper, or offer a choice to each child.

- Place a selection of markers in containers for each child. Two to four markers for each child is enough. If they have different colors, they can trade them.

- Invite a small group of four children to come draw.

- Pass out paper and containers of markers.

- It may help to tape down the paper for the youngest children.

- Reflect their experience by saying what you see, using phrases like, "You made a long red line on your paper."

Limits

- Some very young children will put the markers in their mouths. If offering a teether as a substitute doesn't solve the problem, let them play with something else rather than drawing.

- Decide ahead of time if drawing on their own bodies will be okay.

- Drawing on clothing or others' bodies or clothing is not okay. Use a phrase like, "Markers are for the paper."

Other Things to Think About

- Markers seem basic and unexciting, but you will find toddlers asking for them again and again as they gain small-muscle control of the pens.

- Long paper covering a side of the table provides a community workspace for toddlers to work side by side.

Supporting Play

Imagine being fully involved with the children as you use these strategies, shown in the following scenario, to support children's play.

- Provide opportunities to practice using the markers at varied levels of skill.

Thirty-three-month-old Debbie has requested markers, so caregiver Maryam has gathered a group at the end of the afternoon. Debbie chooses a big piece of paper and quickly sets to work, carefully making a series of vertical lines. Sixteen-month-old Doug heads right for Debbie. Maryam says, "Oh, Doug, this can be your place," setting down a basket of markers and pulling out a chair across from Debbie. Doug sits and chooses a smaller piece of paper. He eagerly pulls the lid off a blue marker and lightly draws it across the paper. He looks to Debbie, and she says, "I'm making a map." He pulls off another lid, makes another mark, and tries to put the lids back on. "Push until you hear the snap," Maryam tells him. She holds his hands in hers when he holds out the pen and a lid. Now he takes them off again, fitting one on the bottom of the marker, as Debbie has done. Two-and-a-half-year-old Yael asks to trade markers with Debbie, saying "I need the red one." She has filled her paper with long horizontal lines. Gazing at them she says, "Snakes! I made snakes!" "It looks like you did," Maryam says.

Walking Boards

Walking boards as part of the basic equipment for outdoor play provide challenge for a wide range of development. Set in a simple pattern on the ground, the boards challenge the children to follow the walking path while staying on the boards. Boards set on tires like balance beams or inclined like ramps offer gravitational challenges to the crawling infant or the newly walking toddler.

What You'll Need

- Smooth 1-by-12-inch or 2-by-12-inch walking boards 4 to 10 feet long. The longer the board, the thicker it should be, so it does not bend or break under the toddlers' weight.

- Tires or other supports.

What to Do

- Set up a pocket of play to include boards connecting areas or equipment in the yard. For example, boards could lead from the cooking area to the trucks, or connect the steps of slides to the place where the slide ends.

- Make sure the ends of the boards meet and are at the same level so children don't trip over a protruding end.

- Offer encouragement and coaching as infants and toddlers crawl on, step onto, or walk along the boards.

Limits

- Consider providing more than one entrance and exit within a path to minimize collisions.

- Use *beep, beep* as the signal that someone wants to pass; facilitate verbal communication.

Other Things to Think About

◻ Try boards that are narrower or wider to let children practice with different challenges.

◻ Provide safety mats or cushions if boards are more than 1 foot off the ground.

Supporting Play

Use these strategies, shown in the following scenario, to support children's play.

◻ Provide opportunities for practice at varied levels of skill.

◻ Promote body awareness by coaching.

An 8-foot board, 2 by 12 inches, extends ramp-like from a tire and rests in the sand area. A 4-foot board, 1 by 12 inches, lies flat on the sand at the bottom of the ramp. Ten-month-old May crawls onto the flat board, then up onto the angled board. Meanwhile, newly walking Mikey approaches the flat board, gingerly negotiates the edge, and steps up onto it. Caregiver Aira notices and says, "You kept your balance, Mikey, as you stepped up onto that board." Nineteen-month-old Matt leans over the tire, placing his hands on the board as he crawls onto the slanted board. He stands up from all fours, gathering speed as he goes down the incline. Aira is there and says, "You ran down off the board." When Matt turns to go up the slide, he begins by crawling. Slowly, Matt moves to a squat. Aira says, "You can straighten your knees if you want to stand up. I'll stay right here."

Boxes

Going beyond pop-up boxes, a collection of boxes or small containers that open in various ways encourages investigation and manual dexterity.

What You'll Need

- Boxes that open in a variety of ways (hinge, lift, twist, slide); for example, matchboxes, cigar boxes, egg cartons, take-out boxes of various kinds, and pastry boxes.

- Open boxes with mix-and-match lids, such as shoe or oatmeal boxes.

- Small items to place in each box.

What to Do

- Set out the collection of boxes on a shelf or table accessible to children. Make sure there are at least two boxes for each child.

- Allow the children to discover the boxes on their own.

- Place small toy animals, key chains, laminated photos or other items inside some of the boxes to motivate toddlers to look inside all of them.

- Respond to requests for help by suggesting they try to open and close the boxes themselves. Use phrases like these: "Try two hands," "Take your time," "Tell me what you want it to do." If possible, do only enough to get the children over the barrier so they can experience their own success.

Limits

- Observe closely for increasing frustration, and offer to put aside the box if the child wants to take a break and try again later.

Other Things to Think About

- Provide a variety of small items for the children to use to fill and dump from boxes, if they wish. Older infants love to put objects into containers. Toddlers love to fill and dump.

Supporting Play

Use these strategies, shown in the following scenario, to support children's play:

- Make room for trial and error and repeated investigation.
- Facilitate problem solving with observation and open-ended questions.

Caregiver Kathy observes as seventeen-month-old Mark picks up a small open-topped box. "Ahhh," he says when he turns it over and a small teddy bear falls out. "You found the bear," Kathy says. Mark puts the bear back into the box, then takes it out with his right hand and looks at the empty box in his left hand. Nineteen-month-old Tal has picked up the bear and puts it in her shoe box. "Ni, ni," she says. Twenty-two-month-old Kitty has gathered the largest box along with a few others around her on the floor. She piles toy animals and the small boxes into the large one. "All in here," she says. "You put the animals and small boxes inside the big one," Kathy reflects. Kitty puts the lid on an oatmeal box and shakes it, grinning. Bobby, sixteen months old, puts a teddy bear inside an oatmeal box, then shakes it, dumping it out. Twenty-one-month-old Wendy is holding an oatmeal box. "What in it?" she asks. "How can you open it to find out?" Kathy asks. Wendy tugs at the lid. "Inside, inside," she says. "You, you," she says, holding it out to Kathy. "I'll help," Kathy says. She shows Wendy how to hook her fingers under the edge of the lid in order to pull it off. "Pull, pull," Wendy says to herself.

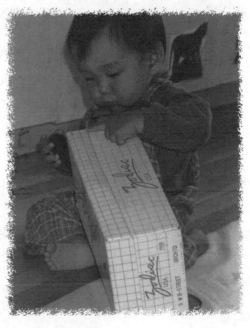

Velcro Balls and Paddles

Older infants and toddlers are fascinated by the effort (and sound!) of sticking and removing balls covered with soft Velcro surfaces. This is an opportunity to begin practicing throwing and catching coordination skills.

What You'll Need

- Velcro-covered paddles and matching balls. These are commercially available, or you can make your own with the following materials:
  - Pieces of Velcro from a fabric store (both hook and loop sides) to cover balls and flat surfaces.
  - Paddles or flat surfaces to cover with the hook side of the Velcro (approximately 6 by 6 inches).
  - Whiffle ball, tennis ball or similar sized balls to cover with loop side of the Velcro.

What to Do

- Place paddles around the yard. Be sure there are enough so interested toddlers can have a choice and taking turns can happen without a long wait (consider having four paddles available for groups of eight toddlers).

- Stick soft Velcro balls to the paddles.

- Put some paddles or big pieces of hooked Velcro mounted on cardboard on a wall or fence as targets. This works best when the Velcro is at the children's height.

- Put up some Velcro at a lower level for infants to stick and remove balls (indoors or outdoors).

- Caregivers can make additional Velcro balls by attaching Velcro strips to tennis balls or whiffle balls.

- Caregivers can model simple throwing and catching: toss a ball at the toddler's paddle, and catch it when the toddler throws it back.

Limits

- If used indoors, set clear limits about not throwing hard things such as blocks. (See "Soft Objects to Throw Indoors" in *Infant and Toddler Experiences*, page 234.)

Other Things to Think About

- The lightweight Velcro balls can be used indoors on a rainy day with a small group of toddlers or older infants.

- Toddlers like just carrying the paddles around.

- Combine this experience with "Hanging Balls Outdoors" (see page 161) by hanging a Velcro covered ball from a string or rope and catching it with a Velcro paddle.

Supporting Play

Use these strategies, shown in the following scenario, to support children's play:

- Provide opportunities for practice at varied levels of skill.

- Make room for trial and error and repeated investigation.

Four sets of Velcro paddles and balls are in the yard. Eighteen-month-old Carmen kneels by one set, holding down the paddle with one hand and pulling off the ball with the other. Seemingly satisfied, she moves to the swing. "Did you find the Velcro balls and paddles?" caregiver Fran asks twenty-two-month-old Vince, as he picks up two paddles and offers one to twenty-six-month-old Omri, who has just thrown a Velcro ball. Omri takes the paddle, and Vince walks off with a paddle and a ball, holding the ball on top of the paddle. Omri retrieves his ball and sticks it to his paddle. Holding the paddle by its strap, he shakes it upside down, then holds it with both hands and shakes it some more. The ball sticks to the paddle. Looking up, he exchanges a smile with Fran, and pulls off the ball and says, "Catch?" holding it up. "Okay, ready," Fran says. Omri throws the ball close to Fran and she catches it. "Are you ready?" she asks. Omri holds out the paddle, wavering a bit, and she throws the ball and he catches it on his paddle.

Ten-month-old Adriana crawls to the wall where a square foot of Velcro material has a Velcro-covered ball stuck to it. From her knees, she pulls the ball off and smiles at the sound. Adriana claps the ball between her hands, then slaps it onto the Velcro. It sticks, and she pulls it off after two attempts. She repeats this focused action four more times.

Tube Rollers

Perfect for early walkers, these pull-along rollers will delight young toddlers. They are light enough to pull and respond with jumpy, bouncy movement that young children love to make and observe.

We first saw this idea in Transition Magician 2, *by Mary Henthorne, Nola Larson, and Ruth Chvojicek.*

What You'll Need

- Heavy-duty cardboard tubes (heavier than paper-towel rolls), such as mailing tubes or tubes from carpet stores or art-paper rolls.
- Cotton string or other soft twine to make a pull string with a handle.

What to Do

- Assemble the rollers ahead of time by threading the string through the tube and tying the ends together. Toddlers can pull the roller by holding onto the string, or you can add a string loop for a handle.
- Assemble some rollers with two different diameters of tubes so that one can fit inside the other.
- Place the rollers in the environment and allow infants and toddlers to discover them.
- Reflect children's interest, adding language and vocabulary words for their actions: *pull, roll, behind, follow, lead.*

Limits

- Rollers with strings are for pulling on the ground or for carrying. Provide alternatives for other actions that may be unsafe, such as swinging or hitting.

Other Things to Think About

- A hard surface is best for the tubes to roll on.

- This works best in an open area so toddlers can safely walk, pull, and look behind to watch their action.

- If there is room indoors, this is a great rainy day experience because it provides a focus for large-muscle play.

- You can use stickers, tape, or markers to decorate the tubes, if you like. This adds to the visual interest as the tube rolls.

- Lightweight cardboard tubes from paper towels or wrapping paper will be short-lived material, but they can be strung together lengthwise for children to pull in a similar fashion.

Supporting Play

Use these strategies, shown in the following scenario, to support children's play:

- Provide opportunities for practice at varied levels of skill.

- Allow innovative use of materials.

Caregiver Bryan watches as infants and toddlers discover the rollers he has put in the environment this afternoon. Thirteen-month-old Edo sits with the tubes vertical to the ground, pulling the smaller tube in and out of the larger one. "Wow, oh wow," two-year-old Bin says, as she picks up the string, holding the rollers off the ground. "Bye-bye," she says, holding the string out from her body so the roller is still off the ground and carrying it as she walks off. Bryan responds by saying, "Bye-bye." Bin lets the roller down and pulls it behind her. Joshua, who is twenty-one months old, observes Edo for a minute before sitting with his tubes. He pulls out the smaller one and reverses it before putting it back in. After repeating this eight times, he states, "Tube play peekaboo with the other!" "It's hiding, just like playing peekaboo," Bryan confirms. Three-year-old Rafael puts the string over his arm and carries off a tube set. "My backpack," he says, striding off.

Water Balls

When toddlers discover these balls that look like, but are very different from, the balls they are familiar with, curiosity is aroused, shared delight ensues, and problem solving occurs. Infants will be surprised when they try to roll them.

What You'll Need

- Identical inflatable beach balls (8 to 10 for twelve toddlers).
- Water.

What to Do

- Fill half the beach balls approximately one-third full of water. Inflate them so they are all of equal size.
- Place them in the environment and let the children discover them.
- Reflect the children's interests.

Limits

- The same limits apply to any ball play: don't throw or drop the balls on some-one who isn't playing. Teaching the use of the word *Ready?* before throwing a ball helps.

Other Things to Think About

- If this is a rainy day experience, consider where to use balls that may leak water.

Supporting Play

Use these strategies, shown in the following scenario, to support children's play:

- Provide choices of materials and time to manipulate them.
- Facilitate problem solving with observation and open-ended questions.

> *Twenty-month-old Zane runs to the beach balls on the grass. He picks up one and throws it. He chooses another, and leans over to pick it up, but his hands slip off it. He leans over again, getting a good grip, and picks it up and drops it. It makes a splashing clunk. Zane laughs. "Water," he says. "Yes, it's filled with water," caregiver Julie says. Zane locates two of the water balls and tries to pick them both up at the same time. He reaches both arms around them from every direction, but he quits after about forty-five seconds. Zane picks up one ball at a time and moves them to a spot on the edge of the grass. He kicks one expertly, maneuvering it like a soccer ball. Thirty-month-old George picks up one of the balls and shakes it near his ear. "This one has water," he announces. Julie says, "You can hear the water inside when you shake it." "Shake, shake, shake," George says. Eighteen-month-old Natalie follows George and picks up one of the balls and drops it. She repeats this about ten times, smiling the whole time.*

Heavy, Light

Toddlers love to test their strength as part of their investigation of gravity. "Heavy, Light" offers toddlers experience with moving, picking up, and carrying different weights.

What You'll Need

- Blocks of assorted sizes and materials, so that blocks that are similar in size and shape are of different weights. For example, offer foam, cardboard, and hollow plastic blocks, even blocks made of milk cartons or other types of boxes and stuffed with newspaper to be sturdy. There should be both large and small blocks in the collection.

What to Do

- Set out the blocks in an area. A low board on grass or sand can act as a stage or building area.
- Allow the toddlers to carry, stack, push, and otherwise safely move the blocks.
- Observe their reaction to the various weights so you can reflect them. Use phrases like these to support toddlers' thinking about *heavy* and *light*:

  You're working very hard.

  That one seems heavier.

  Look how strong you are.

  Can you feel how that one is heavier/lighter?

Limits

- Blocks are not for throwing. Provide lots of balls, especially large, heavier ones, to throw as an alternative.

Other Things to Think About

- Extend opportunities for weight comparison by including different sizes and shapes of each type of block.

- Offer blocks in various shapes and weights to challenge toddlers as they practice building.

Supporting Play

Use these strategies, shown in the following scenario, to support children's play:

- Provide opportunities for practice at varied levels of skill, especially balance, control, and strength.

- Promote body awareness by coaching.

Several toddlers approach the boards where caregiver Jim has placed familiar cardboard blocks and newer foam ones. Two-and-a-half-year-old Andy runs to grab one. After lifting it 2 inches, he drops it. Shaking his head, he looks at Jim and asks, "Whaaat?" Jim answers, "It's heavy. Can you pick it up?" Andy uses both hands to pick it up and carries it to the other end of the board. "You did it," says Jim. When Andy returns for another block, it almost flies out of his hand when he lifts it. "Not heavy," he says. Jim reflects, "That block is not as heavy. It's lighter than the other one you carried." Andy easily moves it to set it on top of the other one. When he returns for more, he tests each block by lifting it a bit. Andy chooses a heavy one to lift onto the other two. "You are strong to be able to carry that heavy block," Jim says. Meanwhile, eighteen-month-olds Kelly and Karen have discovered the foam blocks. Taking them off the board, they flop around and fall. Kelly squats to grab the cylinder with both hands, balancing it upright for ten steps. Karen follows, and they flop them down on the sand side by side. "You did it," Jim comments. Kelly and Karen sit on the cylinders as if they are riding horses.

Gluing Collage on Foil

Younger and older toddlers enjoy using a material for gluing that differs in texture and appearance from regular paper. Foil is shiny on one side and dull on the other. It will support gluing of lightweight items.

Thanks to Johanna Leni for originating this experience.

What You'll Need

- Heavy-duty foil cut into 12-by-15-inch pieces.
- Lightweight collage material, such as string, yarn, tissue paper, scrap paper pieces, cotton balls, or feathers.
- Glue.
- Bowls.
- Brushes.

What to Do

- Invite a small group of toddlers to do some gluing.
- Show them the foil and say something like, "We'll be using foil to glue on instead of paper."
- Give each child her own bowl, glue, and a brush.
- Give each child another bowl with a variety of collage materials in it.
- Respond to any comments about the foil being different from paper used in previous art experiences.

Limits

- Older toddlers may put a lot of glue onto the foil. Just observe and offer another piece of foil.

Other Things to Think About

⬛ Try using foil for other projects, such as painting or taping.

Supporting Play

Use these strategies, shown in the following scenario, to support children's observation and investigation:

⬛ Plan to extend the exploration, using children's interests as a guide.

⬛ Offer information ("Say what you know").

Two-and-a-half-year-old Cecelia and Van go to the table. Sixteen-month-old Paul and twenty-two-month-old Benz go to the shelves to play with toys first.

At the table, Cecelia asks, "What is this?" "This is aluminum foil," responds caregiver Johanna. Cecelia asks, "What are we going to do with this?" "We're going to glue different things onto it," Johanna says. Cecelia gets to work, pausing as she looks closely at the foil. She says, "Johanna, I can see myself." "It's a reflection of you like when you look in a mirror, Cecelia. The foil is shiny," Johanna tells her. Van is brushing glue onto the foil until a good portion of the foil is covered. Then, one by one, he puts pieces of material on it. After five minutes, Paul comes to the table and Johanna supplies him with foil, glue, and collage material. He spreads glue with the brush, grabs a handful of collage material, and dumps it on the foil. He repeats this process. Benz continues playing with the toys on the shelf.

Observation and Experimentation with Water

Sciencing is a term coined by Bev Bos and Michael Leeman in a workshop at the CAEYC Annual Conference. It means "doing science" and may be practiced just like singing, dancing, or painting. In this experience, supply toddlers with materials that respond to water differently, and allow them to practice their observational skills. As caregivers help toddlers articulate their own curiosity and resulting observations, they support toddlers' learning about how to learn.

What You'll Need

- Small blocks of Styrofoam, about 1 inch on a side.

- Small sponges cut into approximately 1-inch squares.

- Packing peanuts made of cornstarch (not the Styrofoam ones).

- Uncooked pasta, such as rotelli, that is a similar size to the packing peanuts.

- Small bowls 6 to 8 inches in diameter, so that pieces of the Styrofoam blocks and the sponges will fit inside.

- Pitcher of water to fill bowls.

- Small (one-cup) pouring pitcher.

- Towels for cleanup.

What to Do

- Gather four older toddlers and introduce the experience by saying something like, "You each have a bowl that you get to fill with water. There are some different materials to put in the water to watch what happens."

- Fill a small pitcher with water and let the toddlers take turns using it to fill their bowls.

- Pass a bowl of Styrofoam blocks, letting each toddler choose one or two.

- Extend the experience by asking open-ended questions like these:

    What happened?

    Is it on top of the water or underneath the water?

- Offer new language and information such as *sinking, floating,* or *dissolving.*

- Repeat the process for each material.

Limits

- Experiment in your own bowl.

- This experience will probably become just water play after 5 or 10 minutes, depending on the group.

- Decide ahead of time how long you will let this go on, or under what circumstances you will start cleaning up.

Other Things to Think About

- Be aware that use of sponges may turn into a cleaning party, distracting children from the observation.

- Have alternative experiences ready for those who don't wish to participate or who dump the water.

- Repeat this experience over time so toddlers can hone their observation skills. Caregivers will see new things too!

Supporting Play

Use these strategies, shown in the following scenario, to support children's curiosity:

- Provide choices of materials and time to manipulate them.

- Validate child's experience ("Say what you see").

- Offer information ("Say what you know").

Caregiver Marilyn has gathered four toddlers to observe what happens. First, they fill their bowls with water. Eighteen-month-old Keishi pours the water out of her bowl as soon as she has filled it. Marilyn suggests she might want to play with the Lego blocks or read a book, and Keishi goes immediately to sit on the pillow with a book. Marilyn continues with the experiment. She passes a bowl of packing peanuts and each toddler adds a few to his bowl. Thirty-five-month-old Jim says, "They're going away, a-going away?" Marilyn comments, "They are dissolving in the water." As the peanuts get limp, Allison says, "Broken, broken." "Where are they?" Marilyn asks after the peanuts have dissolved. Allison says, "Wa-wa." "They're in the water." Marilyn confirms. Allison nods her head, and says, "Right here," pointing at the swirling white thickness in her bowl. Marilyn offers another bowl with sponge pieces in it. Twenty-six-month-old Ruben predicts floating when asked if the sponge would sink or float. Then Julia stands, holding her bowl, and sways. The water moves. "What happened?" she asks. "What did you see?" Marilyn asks. Jade, twenty-nine months old, stands at the table concentrating on her bowl. She takes out the peanuts every few moments. Jade grabs the dissolving peanuts and rubs the goop between her hands. Marilyn asks her, "How does it feel?" Jade offers, "Sticky." She continues to dip other materials into her bowl.

TODDLERS

Make Your Own Playdough!

Toddlers enjoy stirring and pouring real ingredients to make their own play-dough. They can experiment with simple measuring.

What You'll Need

- Flour in large bowl to scoop from.
- Salt in large bowl to scoop from.
- Vegetable oil.
- Water.
- Small plastic pitcher to measure and pour from.
- Plastic bowls 6 to 8 inches in diameter for individual mixing (one per child).
- Small spoons for mixing.
- Measuring cups and spoons.
- Plastic resealable bags for storage.

What to Do

- Work from the following recipe, and have enough of each ingredient for each child to make a bowl of playdough. One cup of flour makes a usable ball of play-dough for one child.

   Uncooked Playdough
   1 cup flour
   ½ cup salt
   1 tablespoon oil
   1 cup water

- Gather four toddlers and explain, "You each get to make playdough. You'll all have a turn."

- Give each child a small mixing bowl and a spoon.

- Use a half-cup measure to scoop the flour and salt first. Say to the children, "We need two scoops flour," and let each scoop the flour from the big bowl into their own bowl.

- When you get to the oil, you can let children use the tablespoon to dip it out of the bowl (tell them they need "one big spoon of oil,") or you can measure two tablespoons of oil into a small pitcher and let them pour it into their bowls.

- Add water the same way that the oil was added.

- After all the ingredients are in the children's bowls, encourage thorough stirring to get all the dry parts mixed. Model scraping the sides of the bowl. Ask, "Do you need more water?"

- Turn the dough out of the bowls and onto the table to knead as soon as the ingredients are mixed. The children may want more flour.

- Have resealable plastic bags ready in case children want to take their playdough home. Tape the bag shut and write the child's name on it.

Limits

- Say that the children should work on thei own playdough, and be prepared with words to use with children who are attracted to others' playdough ("Thanks for offering to help; I think she wants to do it herself)."

- Playdough is for hands and fingers, not fc eating. Model pretend play by holding playdough away from your mouth and making smacking noises.

Other Things to Think About

- This playdough is perishable and will spoil if left at room temperature.

- Children with cooking experience will jump right in. Others may wish to watch for a while or for the first time.

Supporting Play

Use these strategies, shown in the following scenario, to support children's exploration:

- Plan to extend the exploration, using children's interest as a guide.
- Offer information ("Say what you know").

When four toddlers enter the art room, there are bowls and spoons on the table. Caregiver Jan explains that they will be making their own playdough, and that everyone will get a turn. "We need to mix flour, salt, water, and oil to make it." In turn, the toddlers scoop flour and salt, then use a small pouring pitcher to add water and a tablespoon of oil. They all are stirring the dry flour immediately, and Jan says, "Try to keep the flour in the bowl." As the wet ingredients are mixed, Jan moves around to each toddler, commenting, "Do you cook at home? I see you are stirring that efficiently." Ari answers "Eggs." "Oh, you whip eggs." Two-year-old Ari tips the bowl to whip the ingredients. Julia is spontaneously singing the "Stirring the Brew" Halloween song. Jan says, "Waly, yours is ready to play with. Let's turn it out onto the table." Thirty-month-old Phil says, "I'm making pizza!" as he pounds the dough. Nineteen-month-old Patricia is drawing designs in the flour on the table with her finger. Julia goes to the playdough drawer for a roller.

Fun with Flashlights

When toddlers can hold their own small flashlight, they have fun turning it on and off and investigating moving light and shadow.

What You'll Need

- Four to six flashlights (4 to 6 inches long—the kind that uses one AA battery).
- Extra batteries and bulbs.

What to Do

- Plan for this experience to take place in a dark or slightly dark room or on a dark day with the lights off. Compare the flashlight effects with the room lights on or off.

- Distribute the flashlights, using the word *flashlight* to expand children's available stock of words. Use a phrase like this one: "Today we have some flashlights. Let's see how they work."

- Let children know when you will turn the room lights out since young children may be startled by sudden dark, even with the flashlights. Use a phrase like this: "I'm going to turn the light out now. It will be darker."

- Respond to requests for help turning the flashlights on and off, and validate their comments about the light.

Limits

- The flashlights are used to direct the light, not to pound, hit, or shine in people's eyes. (This is not usually a major problem since light is so fascinating for toddlers.)

Other Things to Think About

- Younger children seem to need to touch the wall with the flashlight.

- Plan multiple experiences with flashlights and other light sources. For example, use a slide projector for making shadows low on the wall. (See "Shadow Puppets," on page 149.)

- Older toddlers might hold their flashlights for others to make shadows on the wall.

- Try this experience outdoors at the end of a dark winter day.

Supporting Play

Use these strategies to deepen children's experience with the flashlights.

- Validate child's experience.

- Offer information ("Say what you know").

The toddlers love seeing that flashlights can really light their way. They set out by holding a caregiver's hand, then race off. It is particularly fun to look at a mirror in the dark with a flashlight. Garrett puts one under his "bucket head hat" so the light shines through it. He views himself in the mirror, smiling with satisfaction, "I did it." Later the caregivers find out that Garrett's dad has a head lamp he uses when camping. Dan crouches down to make repeating circles over the sidewalk with the flashlight. He watches it very closely.

Sprouting Seeds

Toddlers' connection with the concept of growing food to eat may be initiated by sprouting seeds. This process takes several days and offers opportunities to stimulate all the senses.

What You'll Need

- Seeds such as alfalfa, lentil, or mung beans.
- Clear plastic jars or containers, such as a mayonnaise or peanut butter jar.
- Trays and cheesecloth or paper towels.
- Small bowls or containers.
- Water.
- Small pitcher.
- Strainer or colander with small holes.

What to Do

- If you have never sprouted seeds, you may want to try it at home to plan the timing. Different seeds have varying germination rates and require different temperatures. The goal is to sprout and eat the seeds within a caregiving week (Monday to Friday).
- Gather a small group of toddlers, explaining that they are going to grow some seeds.
- Have a few seeds in a small bowl for each toddler.
- Allow the toddlers to feel, manipulate, and smell the seeds, but tell them to save eating until after the seeds grow.
- Use descriptive language in talking about the seeds, as well as the names of the kinds of seed you have: soft, hard, smaller than, larger than, brown, yellow, round, flat, alfalfa, mung, wheat, and so forth.

- Have each child pour or drop their seeds into the clear plastic container. (Use one container for each small group of toddlers, and write the children's names on it.)

- Offer about a quarter cup of water in a pitcher for each child to pour into the jar to water their seeds.

- Let the seeds soak overnight and pour the water out in the morning.

- The seeds need to be rinsed with clean water once a day. Pour water into the jar, and pour the water and seeds out into a strainer. Shake them gently to get most of the water out, then pour them back into the jar. Keep the jar of seeds in a dark place (like a cupboard).

- Each day, take a few sprouted seeds from the strainer and put them onto paper towels on trays so that the toddlers can feel, smell, and see them and talk about how they have changed. (The rest go back into the jar to continue growing.)

- Each day, further observations can be made as the plants grow.

- Sprouts may usually be eaten in two to four days. Toddlers can taste what they have grown by itself, or you can add the sprouts to soups, salads, or sandwiches, or use them as a topping along with cream cheese on a cracker. (Try to incorporate eating the sprouts into a snack or mealtime.)

Limits

- In a small group, this new experience will be fascinating enough that you will probably need few limits. Some toddlers may need reminding, "These seeds are for touching and looking at now. They will be ready to eat in a few days."

- Provide an alternate experience for those children who are not interested at this time.

Other Things to Think About

- Mixing seeds of various sizes and germinating times provides comparison for detailed observation.

- Older toddlers may stick with the whole process. Younger toddlers will treat it like water play.

- It may surprise you how many of the toddlers actually like eating the sprouts!

Supporting Play

Use these strategies, shown in the following scenario, to support children's investigation with their senses and their interest in knowledge:

- Provide choices of materials and time to manipulate them.

- Share your interests ("Say who you are").

> *Caregiver Beth has planned a seed-sprouting experience. Four toddlers sit around a table, each with a bowl in front of them with a variety of seeds in it. "What?" "Brown," "Green," and "What to do?" are some of the comments from the two-and-a-half-year-olds. "We're going to grow these seeds and eat the sprouts," Beth explains. "First, we need to water them. This will be your jar." She writes the children's names on the jar. "Put your seeds inside the jar, and then we'll water them," she says. Each toddler pours out their bowl of seeds into the jar. Then each toddler pours about a quarter cup of water into the jar from a small pouring pitcher that Beth fills. Later, upon returning to the room, Ramon says, "Where are the seeds? I lost them. Oh, there they are, we watered them." "Yes, and we will again tomorrow," Beth tells him.*
>
> *After three days, some seeds show green sprouts, and others have leaves. After rinsing them, the toddlers inspect a few kept out on a paper towel. August asks, "Eat?" Beth says, "Yes." August eats them and has more. "I see you like the sprouts. I like them in my salad or on a sandwich. They're healthy for your body."*

Making Pudding

Older toddlers can mix their own instant pudding to provide a snack. Cooking and eating are social pleasures for toddlers that can be the basis for building relationships.

What You'll Need

- Instant pudding mix.
- Milk.
- Spoons and bowls for entire group.
- Larger bowl (to measure out of).
- Measuring cups.
- Small plastic pitcher.
- 8-ounce liquid measuring cup.

What to Do

- You may want to experiment ahead of time to determine the approximate ratio of powder to milk necessary to make a thick pudding.
- Gather a group of no more than four toddlers at a time.
- Explain that they are going to make their own snack today.
- Wash hands.
- Distribute spoons and bowls.
- Have each toddler scoop up a quarter cup of pudding mix from the big bowl and pour it into her own bowl.
- Pour about a half cup of milk into a small pitcher for the toddlers to pour over the pudding mix in their bowls.

- Stirring may be encouraged with a song, such as "Stirring and stirring and stirring the pudding." Or use a chant, such as "Milk in the batter, milk in the batter!" from Maurice Sendak's *In the Night Kitchen.* Toddlers may spontaneously make these connections.

- If mixing is vigorous, the pudding will set quickly. A related story about cooking could be read while you wait less than five minutes for the pudding to thicken enough to eat. Or take advantage of this time for conversation.

Limits

- Cooking is fun when toddlers are focused. They may need reminding that the pudding stays in the bowl to be stirred.

- Provide other things to do when a child loses interest or is finished.

Other Things to Think About

- Combine with "Cutting Bananas" (see page 166) to make banana pudding, or use other fruit. Fruit could be cut up while the pudding sets.

- Ask parents for family recipes for simple pudding dishes.

Supporting Play

Bear in mind the role of cooking and eating in families and cultures as you use these strategies, which are also shown in the following scenario:

- Affirm mutual interests to encourage interdependence.

- Affirm family culture.

The toddlers are excited to be doing real cooking. Jeffrey, thirty-three months old, says, "I stir, stir." Caregiver Taphne says, "We'll all get to stir our own pudding. First, let's measure the powder mix." Jeff scoops and pours into his bowl and immediately begins stirring. "Try to keep it in the bowl while the others measure their mix," Taphne tells him. Joanie is next, and she easily scoops and pours. At twenty-six months old, she is an experienced cook. "I make pancakes with Daddy," she says. "It must be fun to cook together at home," Taphne replies. Twenty-seven-month-old Han and thirty-month-old Thong scoop and pour with concentration. Next, Taphne says, "This is the milk. When it mixes with the powder, it makes pudding." She pours half a cup into a pouring pitcher for each child, and they pour it into their bowls. Now Jeffrey really mixes. "Makin' pudding," he says. Taphne points out, "There's some dry mix not yet mixed in. Try scraping around the edges of the bowl." Han is slightly smiling with the addition of the milk. Thong says, "Milk for the morning cake!" Taphne says, "Oh, that's from the book In the Night Kitchen. *You remembered it. We could read that after the pudding is mixed. After the book, the pudding will be ready to eat."*

Choo-Choo

The immediate environment may provide inspiration for spontaneous games initiated by the children. At our center, a commuter train runs close by. In this child-initiated game, children are the engines of a train and break away from the rest of the train. The adult playfully chases them and tries to catch them.

Thanks to Brenda Ellis for following the children's lead to create this experience.

What You'll Need

No materials needed for this experience.

What to Do

- Clear the space of any obstacles children may run into, such as trikes, cars, or pull toys.

- Children start off by holding hands with the caregiver and other children to form a circle or straight line.

- Everyone moves like a train, starting off slowly and chanting "Choo, choo, woo, woo."

- When the children are ready, the engines (that is, all the children) break off and start running, and the caregiver playfully chases them.

Limits

- As they run, help children be aware of others to prevent collisions.

Other Things to Think About

- Other environmental elements might give rise to child-initiated games, such as sirens, fog horns, planes flying overhead, elevators, squirrels, birds, or elements of weather.

Supporting Play

Use these strategies, shown in the following scenario, to be available to children so authentic connection can take place:

- Slow the pace; be available.

- Affirm mutual interests to encourage interdependence.

Molly sees Eleni and says, "There's the engine." Eleni looks at the caregiver, Brenda, who makes her right hand available and says, "Choo, choo." Brenda lets Eleni grab her left ring finger. Molly grabs Brenda's right hand. And Eleni grabs Molly's right hand to form a circle. Brenda says, "Choo-choo, choo-choo, woo, woo!" They pretend they are a train for one or two minutes; then Eleni walks backward three steps and releases Brenda's finger. She starts running, with Molly immediately following her. Brenda chases after them and says, "Oh, no! The engines are getting away. I have to get the engines." They run together on the circular path around the grass. While they are running, Tara, Arend, Chris, Rich, and Tevis join in. Molly and Eleni laugh together with glee as they trot away from Brenda.

Parachute and Ball Play

Connecting with friends all holding a parachute and working toward a common goal of moving balls on the parachute offers toddlers practice in teamwork. Interdependence is evident as they can see how movement in one part of the parachute moves the balls to another part.

What You'll Need

- Parachute or large piece of lightweight fabric, 10 feet in diameter.

- Lightweight balls of various sizes.

- Three caregivers for every eight to twelve toddlers.

- Open space to unfold and move the parachute and for children to run around and under it safely.

What to Do

- Caregivers strategically place themselves at regular intervals around the parachute, helping toddlers find a handle if they want one.

- Practice a few up-and-down arm movements, working together if possible. Verbalize *up and down.*

- Put balls of various weights and sizes into the middle of the parachute; encourage moving together, up and down. Older toddlers may be asked to get a ball and throw it on the parachute. (Three or four balls at a time is sufficient.)

- Observe and say what you see: "Balls rolling," "Parachute billowing," "Up and down."

Limits

- Pulling down, walking on, or sitting on top of the parachute stops the game. Have other large pieces of fabric available to sit on.

Other Things to Think About

- Note that the easiest way to introduce a parachute is with everyone standing and holding the edges. If you sit around it, toddlers will just crawl on top of it.

- Older infants enjoy crawling under the parachute while it's billowing up and down.

- This is a focused large-muscle experience, useful for short time intervals, such as ten minutes before snack.

Supporting Play

Use these strategies, shown in the following scenario, to support children's play:

- Affirm mutual interests to encourage interdependence.

The yard is busy with twelve toddlers (eighteen to thirty-three months old) and three infants who are visiting outdoors. As ball play on the grass winds down, one of the caregivers pulls out the parachute. "Let's all play with the balls on the parachute," she says. Toddlers run to grab a handle, and two other caregivers space themselves around, assisting the toddlers. Leeza, who was previously playing with a ball, throws one onto the center of the elevated parachute. As the caregivers model up *and* down, *verbalizing it as well, the ball rolls around the parachute. "It's riding the parachute!" Garret says. "Who's going to put more balls on the parachute?" "Now there are six balls in there." "We're moving the balls together. Uh-oh, there goes one," one of the caregiver says as it rolls off the side. An infant crawls under the parachute and sits smiling and wide-eyed, watching the parachute move above his head. "In two minutes we'll put the parachute away and have snack," the caregiver says.*

Real Keys on Key Rings

Real keys that are no longer used by adults provide an enticing imitative experience for toddlers. They love to carry them around and practice using in a keyhole or any hole and use their imagination to go "bye-bye." Toddlers also practice strategies for conflict resolution as they learn to trade or take turns with the keys.

What You'll Need

- Many keys on brightly colored key rings. Key rings must be strong enough to not separate into pieces that children could swallow or choke on.

What to Do

- Get old keys donated from a locksmith or request the keys and key rings from the center's community.
- Seed the environment indoors and out with the keys on the key rings.
- Allow the toddlers to discover the keys.
- Facilitate taking turns and trading when one child wants a key that someone else is using.
- Brightly colored key rings are easy to find when they are dropped.
- Caregiver can model looking for another set of keys by walking and looking around the ground or floor, saying something like, "Let's look for another key chain together."

Limits

- Keys are for holding in your hand, putting in your pocket, or practicing in a key hole or any hole. Keys are not for chewing.
- Provide teethers for chewing.

Other Things to Think About

- Playing with real keys is so fun and reality-based for toddlers that a program can never have too many available. They are a connection with objects of importance to special adults in their lives.

- Keys do get lost in the sand, go home in pockets, or just disappear over time.

Supporting Play

Use these strategies, shown in the following scenario, to support children's play:

- Affirm mutual interests to encourage interdependence.

- Help children learn to resolve conflicts by facilitating trading and taking turns.

A new quantity of keys on key rings with little cars and plastic hooks are seeded on shelves in the loft room. After nap time, twenty-month-old Nadav spies several keys right away and scoops up three in his hand with a big smile. He heads for a keyhole, dropping two to the floor as he selects a key with a green car. Twenty-two-month-old Mariko watches Nadav from the couch, sees the two keys drop to the floor, and goes to pick them up. Nadav turns his head from the keyhole, sees Mariko now holding the keys he dropped, and yells, "Mine, mine!" Caregiver Nannette intercedes before Nadav grabs the keys from Mariko: "You did have those keys, Nadav, but remember you let them drop to the floor. It's Mariko's turn with these. You have the key with a green car. I can tell you really want those keys. You can offer to trade with Mariko or you can wait for your turn when she's finished." Nannette models trading for Mariko and Nadav. Mariko replies, "No, yo' turn next," as she walks to a keyhole. Nadav walks to another keyhole. Nannette says, "Look, you are both playing with the keys."

Soft Puppets

Younger toddlers are fascinated by a "talking" hand with a puppet on it. Older toddlers want to wear the puppet and make the sounds themselves. Caregivers can facilitate the use of this prop at each child's developmental level, expanding their creative expression, self-concept, and autonomy.

What You'll Need

- Socks to use as puppets, or homemade or commercially made animal puppets that fit toddler hands.

- Low table for a stage-like area.

- Mirror mounted on a vertical surface.

What to Do

- Tip over a low table onto its long edge for toddlers to kneel behind like a stage. Or try it in front of a mirror.

- Invite a small group of toddlers to the puppet show.

- Show the puppets and let the children each choose one.

- Discuss the identities of their puppets as you help the children place them on their hands.

- One at a time, invite toddlers to go behind the table to tell the others about their puppets. Use phrases like these to encourage children's puppet shows:

    It's our turn to be the audience.

    We watch and listen. And applaud!

    Please tell us about your puppet.

    Please tell us your story.

    How does your story begin?

    Then what happens?

    Thank you for giving us a puppet show.

- Support children who don't wish to be in the spotlight and those who might want to try it together.

Limits

- Prepare the children for transition time. For example, "When you finish with your puppet, please return it to the basket and choose a book or toy from the shelf."

Other Things to Think About

- Socks are relatively easy for young children to get onto their hands. Assist as they need help.

- If you want to be more elaborate, offer glue and collage materials the day before for toddlers to decorate their sock puppets. (See "Flannel Board" in *Infant and Toddler Experiences,* page 169.) Stuff socks with cardboard when gluing items to them. Then the puppet sock is ready for a show.

Supporting Play

Use these strategies, shown in the following scenario, to support children's development of self-concept and autonomy:

- Be predictable and consistent in meeting children's needs.

- Slow the pace; be available ("Be an island").

- Teach taking turns and trading.

Today the toddlers will get to play with the puppets they made the day before. Caregiver Dawn explains to a group of four toddlers, "We will take turns being the audience and showing our puppets. Let's all sit in the audience chairs. Here, Dejon. This is the puppet you made yesterday." Thirty-four-month-old Dejon puts the puppet on his hand. Dawn invites him to stand behind the table, holding up his puppet. "Please tell us about your puppet, Dejon," she says, adding, "What is its name?" when Dejon doesn't respond. "Name Bugs," Dejon says. "Oh, and what does Bugs like?" Dawn asks. "Pizza!" says Dejon. The audience laughs, which encourages Dejon to say, "French fries!" He's laughing so hard that Dawn begins the applause. "Thank you, Dejon and Bugs. Now its Miri's turn." Miri says, "Goin' on a train." The audience all waves good-bye.

Shadow Puppets

Toddler experimentation with light, dark, and shadow may be extended through the experience of shadow puppets for older toddlers. They are so fascinated by observing the source of light and projected images on a wall that they soon learn to make the shadows themselves.

What You'll Need

- Bright light source, such as an empty slide projector.
- White sheet or light-colored blank wall.
- Low table to define space for toddlers to be behind.
- Various shaped cardboard pieces (geometric shapes or irregular), up to 6 by 9 inches.
- Stiff cardboard pieces for handles, approximately 2 by 12 inches long.
- Stapler.

What to Do

- Have the light source and wall space set up and ready. If toddlers do not have experience with making hand shadows, let them do that first.
- Tip over a low table for the toddlers to kneel behind so their puppet shadows are visible on the wall or sheet as if they are on the "stage" of the table.
- Invite a small group of toddlers (no more than four) to make their own shadow puppets.
- Allow them to choose a shape, discussing with them what it reminds them of. Write their names on their shape.
- Help the children staple the shape to a handle, holding their hands in yours so they feel the pressure necessary to staple.
- Model how to kneel behind the table, and tell them when you are going to turn out the room lights and turn on the light source ("I'm going to turn out the big lights now").

- Say what you see, describing the actions of the puppets and the shadows you see on the wall. Ask open-ended questions: "What do you think it looks like?" "What do you think they're doing?" Reflect and acknowledge all answers as acceptable.

Limits

- Puppets are for holding and making the shadows or using as props in conversations.
- Provide alternatives for large-muscle exercise, such as swinging and throwing balled-up socks.

Other Things to Think About

- This experience may work best by playing with the light and shadows first, then making the puppets to extend the children's experience.
- Extend this experience to shadows seen outdoors on a sunny day.

Supporting Play

Use these strategies, shown in the following scenario, to support children's play as they connect around a common experience:

- Be predictable and consistent in meeting children's needs.
- Affirm mutual interests to encourage interdependence.

Yesterday the toddlers enjoyed doing fingerplays in front of the light. They watched their hands and caregiver Don's hands making shadows on the wall. Today they're going to make shadow puppets on handles. With the materials ready, making the puppets goes quickly. Each toddler chooses a shape from a variety. Don has organized it so the focus is still on the making of shadows. Jenny, thirty months old, says, "Moon," and chooses a crescent shape. Don encourages her to feel the push of the stapler when he staples it to a stick. Thirty-two-month-olds Charlie and Jonathan both want a spiral shape they call a "snake." "You both think that spiral looks like a snake!" Don says. He staples one to a stick for each boy. Kim, thirty-five months old, points at a shape and says, "Triangle." When they are ready behind the stage, Don says he's going to "turn out the big light and turn the projector light on." "Hold up your puppets," Don advises. "If you make them dance a bit you can see which one is yours." He waits for a minute for the toddlers to make the connection. "Please tell us about yours, Kim," asks Don. "House, it's a house," she says. "It does look like a house with a pointy roof," Don comments.

TODDLERS

Papier-Mâché

The feel of the wet wheat paste and dry newspapers gives older toddlers an interesting sensory experience. The planned product, a usable ball, entices young children to look forward to something.

What You'll Need

- Newspaper torn into strips approximately 2 by 3 to 6 inches, 75 to 100 strips for
  each 8-to-10-inch ball.

- Old, partially deflated balls or heavy-duty balloons partially blown up to approximately 8 inches in diameter.

- Dishwashing tub for newspaper pieces.

- Flour and water to make wheat paste (or purchased wheat paste if you can find it
  at wallpaper or craft stores).

- Four 6-inch bowls to mix paste in.

- Low small table or workspace for four toddlers to stand around in order to work
  together.

- Smocks for children, if desired.

- Protective floor covering, if necessary.

- Large wet and dry towels for cleanup of children.

What to Do

- It is easier for everyone if all materials are prepared ahead of time:
  - Tear paper strips and place in tub for all to use.
  - Blow up balloons or have the balls ready. (One balloon or ball for each small
    group.)
  - Cover floor or workspace, if necessary.
  - Mix paste in small bowls. Mix extra to refill bowls.

- Have an alternative experience available for those who want to wait or watch before participating. For example, cover another table with paper and put out markers to use.

- Gather a small group of toddlers, telling them what you'll be doing while pushing up their sleeves, putting on smocks, or removing shirts.

- Show them the balloon: "We're going to make it into a ball," or "This ball is tired. We can make a better ball by covering it with wet paper strips."

- Demonstrate that the paper strips need to be dipped in the paste, then stuck on the ball by laying it over the surface and smoothing it. (The children will try it without the paste at first.) A few strips at a time can be placed in the middle of the table (from the supply in the tub), to encourage doing one strip at a time.

- Some toddlers won't like the feel of the paste. They can watch or do the alternative experience. They are welcome to return.

- As more strips are applied, it becomes more obvious to say, "Let's cover all the red part" (or whatever color the ball or balloon is).

- The caregiver can hold the ball steady, respond to questions, and comment on progress: "You covered the red part! Can you find another spot? See how it sticks with the paste on? How does it feel?"

- Some toddlers may just fingerpaint with the paste on a corner of the table.

- Let children know it's almost time to clean up when you see the ball or balloon is almost covered: "We'll clean up in two minutes with the towels. The ball needs to dry before we can use it. Tomorrow we'll check it to see if it is dry."

Limits

- Paste may be explored with hands, but leave it on the table, not in a friend's hair or clothes.

Other Things to Think About

- Try to help toddlers focus on the technique and on solving the problem of covering the surface.

- A thin layer of papier-mâché will dry overnight. Exposure to a heat vent or a hair dryer will speed the drying process so that toddlers can follow the continuity of the project and enjoy the fruits of their experience.

After their initial experience with the medium, older toddlers may be interested in doing all the steps, from the beginning to end; for example, planning what to make or what shape to cover, tearing the paper, mixing the paste, and building up layers of papier-mâché on the chosen object.

Supporting Play

Use these strategies, shown in the following scenario, to help children integrate their skills:

- Allow for innovative use of materials.

- Facilitate problem solving with observation and open-ended questions.

Caregiver Janice invites toddlers to "come make a new ball." "This balloon can be a ball; we can work together," she tells them. "Dip the paper strips in the paste and layer them on the ball to make it stronger," Janice says while demonstrating. Thirty-three-month-old Robin becomes entranced, concentrating hard and carefully pasting one strip at a time. She points out uncovered areas to two-and-a-half-year-old Dorian, who is "washing" her hands with the paste. Thirty-four-month-old Shoudan grabs handfuls of paper to place on the ball at once, in a "get it done" way. In contrast, twenty-two-month-old Omri retreats to the markers for five minutes before poking at the paste and putting three strips on the ball. Eve brings in a leaf and talks to Robin about incorporating it into the covering.

The next day, Janice and the toddlers investigate the finished balls and talk about how different they feel. "Is it hard or soft?" "Wet or dry?" "Let's try rolling it on the floor," says Janice, and the toddlers sit to roll a ball between outstretched legs. They take time in between turns to knock on the ball and pull at it a bit. "Remember when it was sticky and wet? You put the paper strips on to cover the red balloon," Janice reminds them.

The toddlers especially enjoy using the ball outdoors, most choosing to kick it like a soccer ball. Days later, after Janice has mended one of the papier-mâché balls by putting tape where it lost its covering, Robin wants to get tape to cover a hole that a bird pecked in another ball that one of the teachers found up in a tree.

Colored Bubble Art

Many toddlers are familiar with bubbles being blown in the yard or at parties. This experience gives them the opportunity to try it as an art experience. Older toddlers can learn to control their breath to blow bubbles in order to see the effect of the colored bubbles blown onto paper.

Thanks to Johanna Leni for originating this experience.

What You'll Need

- Small bubble containers that are no-spill and come with wands (enough for each child to have one).
- Extra bubble solution or extra prefilled bottles.
- Food coloring or washable liquid paint (food coloring may stain clothes).
- White paper.

What to Do

- Mix the color into the bubble solution and fill the no-spill containers.
- Gather a small group of older toddlers and explain that today they get to blow colored bubbles onto the paper.
- Give each child a bottle of bubble solution and a piece of paper on the table.
- Each child blows bubbles onto the paper, watching them pop and observing the marks they make on the paper.
- Respond to children's comments, refill or exchange bottles if necessary, and facilitate trading colors as toddlers request.

Limits

- Bubbles are meant to be blown onto the paper, not other people.

Other Things to Think About

- This experience is easily moved outdoors. Use larger paper mounted on a fence or wall, and take wind direction into consideration.

- Bottles and wands could be bigger for outdoor use.

Supporting Play

Use these strategies, shown in the following scenario, to support children's efforts:

- Make room for trial and error and repeated investigation.

- Allow for innovative use of materials.

Helen has gathered four toddlers indoors to blow bubbles for an art experience. She gives them each a bubble bottle and wand, suggesting that they can blow the bubbles onto the paper. Thirty-three-month-old Emma blows the bubbles, stopping to see them land on the table and on the paper. She repeats, blowing a little at a time and checking to see where they land. "There's one on the paper, Emma," Helen comments. Twenty-nine-month-old Rob blows down toward the paper, watching the bubbles splat. He repeats this action a dozen times, until his paper is filled with colored evidence of his bubble blowing. Thirty-month-old Itai could not get any on the paper but is having fun blowing the bubbles anyway. Eighteen-month-old Celeste sits quickly, saying "Paiting," and proceeds to use the wand as a brush, dipping it into the bottle and rubbing colors onto the paper.

Hammering

Older toddlers are attracted to using tools such as small hammers. They are able to focus and practice their eye-hand coordination by hammering golf tees into thick Styrofoam. The combination of challenge and probable success is a perfect example of optimal stress.

What You'll Need

- Small hammers that look real but are made out of plastic. Or use plastic mallets from pound-a-ball sets.

- Golf tees.

- Styrofoam rectangles or cubes at least 3 inches thick.

What to Do

- Gather materials.

- Gather a small group of older toddlers.

- Stress that safety and proper use is important when using tools such as hammers.

- Explain that the hammers are *only* for hammering the tees into the Styrofoam.

- Help a toddler poke a tee into the Styrofoam so it stands by itself to be hammered.

- You may need to show the toddlers how to hold the hammer (at the end of the handle), and suggest they look at the tee (what they are trying to hit).

- You may begin by holding the hammer with the child, your hand over hers, so that she gets the feel. (Some toddlers will refuse help, and that's okay.)

Limits

- Explain that the hammers are *only* for hammering the tees into the Styrofoam.

- Provide alternatives, as this may be a brief experience for younger toddlers. A pound-a-ball game might be a good alternative.

Other Things to Think About

- Older toddlers often want to do this themselves, so your assistance may not be welcomed. Be prepared to practice optimal stress by helping only as requested or as much as necessary to get the toddler over the barrier.

Supporting Play

Use these strategies, shown in the following scenario, to extend toddlers' coordination:

- Provide opportunities for practice at varied levels of skill.

- Promote body awareness by coaching.

Caregiver Danielle shows a small group of toddlers the golf tees and hammers they will use today. "You can pound the balls or do markers at the table until it's your turn," she tells them. Two-and-a-half-year-old Ron takes the hammer for his turn, and Danielle asks the other toddlers, "It's okay to watch, but please stay back from the table." Ron holds the hammer in both hands, guiding rather than pounding the hammer. Danielle encourages a freer motion, but Ron says, "Mysef." "Three more tries and it's Sally's turn," Danielle says. Ron pushes a tee in with his hand. Thirty-five-month-old Sally expertly takes the hammer and matches the head to the top of a tee. She pounds, and the tee goes in after three swings. "Again," she says. "There are three more tees, then it will be Janie's turn," says Danielle. Sally hammers with one hand, the other steadying the tee. She easily hammers in three more tees. Meanwhile, Ron is vigorously pounding the pound-a-ball set.

Hanging Balls Outdoors

Hanging balls on ropes or cords from trees offers the opportunity for toddlers to practice hand-eye coordination. Toddlers can throw the ball and catch it when it comes back or hit it safely with implements.

What You'll Need

- Small whiffle balls (about 3 inches in diameter).
- Sturdy rope or cord.
- Duct tape.

What to Do

- Attach balls to ropes, taping them if necessary.
- Hang balls from sturdy tree branches or other support at approximately 6 inches higher than the tallest toddler.
- Hang two or three balls so there is an option for more than one toddler to do this experience simultaneously. Space them far enough apart so the swinging ball will not hit a child playing with another nearby.
- Be sure to set up this experience outside of traffic areas or group areas.
- Allow children to discover the swinging balls.

Limits

- Few limits are necessary if this experience is set up safely.
- If children pull down or hang on the balls or rope, say something like, "The ball is for throwing and catching. Can you catch it after you throw it?"

Other Things to Think About

▪ Toddlers will use implements—like shovels—to hit and catch the balls. This is probably safe when others are not too close. Decide ahead of time what's okay, and help children keep an eye on what's around them. Remember that the shovels, funnels, or other implements may be used in a constructive manner to practice and gain hand-eye coordination. Using the implements to hit the ball is also an alternative to pounding or hitting inappropriate objects or people.

Supporting Play

Use these strategies, shown in the following scenario, to enhance toddlers' experience of this creative challenge:

▪ Provide opportunities for practice at varied levels of skill.

▪ Allow for innovative use of materials.

Thirty-month-old Gene exclaims, "There's a ball! Ong ahoo tree." "Yes, there's a ball hanging from the tree," caregiver Peter affirms. Gene bats it with his hand, watching it swing. After five tries, he is ready to bat it back with his hand as it comes to him. Gene practices a full five minutes, reluctantly going in for lunch and a nap. "I saw you were really working hard on hitting the ball. It will still be up after your nap," Peter tells him. After a nap, Gene heads straight for the hanging ball. This time he is joined by Ash and Don. Younger, at twenty-three months, they tend to throw the ball and duck as it returns. Gene moves over to the other ball, renegotiating the swinging ball at this slightly different height. After two tries, he bats it gracefully. Sixteen-month-old Caryn simply stands, holding the ball in one hand and moving it back and forth. Twenty-month-old Claudia holds it with two hands, then lets go.

Ramps for Wheeled Vehicles

Using large pieces of exterior plywood, make angled ramps for toddlers to use wheeled vehicles on. This allows them to feel the push when they go up, and the pull when they come down.

What You'll Need

- Exterior plywood in 4-by-4-foot pieces. Have two or three.

- Tires, milk crates, railroad ties, or other supports approximately 6 to 10 inches off the ground.

What to Do

- Set up shallow ramps by propping the pieces of plywood on the supports. Make sure they are supported across the whole top edge.

- Allow the toddlers to discover the ramps. Let them ride or push wheeled toys up and down the ramps.

Limits

- For safety, enforce a one-way rule to minimize collisions. Have the children go up only one side and down the other.

- No collisions or crashing on purpose.

Other Things to Think About

- Help younger toddlers see and negotiate the edges when they walk or ride the ramp.

- Smaller ramps can be set up to use with toy cars, trucks, or any small wheeled toy.

Supporting Play

Use these strategies, shown in the following scenario, to help toddlers gain experience with the power of gravity:

- Make room for trial and error and repeated investigation.

- Facilitate problem solving with observation and open-ended questions.

- Promote body awareness by coaching.

Armando has set up the yard using the idea of ramps. He has made two pockets of play with different sizes of boards used for the ramps. The smaller board rests on a milk crate with a crate full of small wheeled vehicles beside it. Two-and-a-half-year-olds Pamela and Neil head directly for it as they come outdoors after snack. "My turn," Neil calls, and Pamela positions herself at the bottom of the ramp to catch the trucks. Thirty-five- and thirty-two-month-olds Bhan and Thomas race for the larger ramp. Standing over their trikes, they walk them up one side of the ramp, sitting and holding up their feet to ride down the other side. Armando points out that twenty-month-old Meli wants to try it, and they let her get in line on the up side of the ramp. Armando coaches her up and down, catching the cart she's pushing as it careens off on the down side. She tries to go up the down side, and Armando helps her get around for another try. Bhan and Thomas spend twenty minutes repeating the ride, saying "Whee," as they ride down, which is evidence of their exhilaration. Perhaps it is similar to swinging and other experiences with gravity.

Cutting Bananas

Using plastic picnic knives, toddlers can cut up their own bananas for eating immediately or for using in a pudding or salad.

What You'll Need

- Plastic picnic knives (having enough for the entire group will save washing between small groups).

- Enough bananas for each toddler to have about a third of a banana.

What to Do

- Wash the bananas if toddlers will peel them themselves. (This is necessary because of the high rate of pesticide use on bananas.)

- Gather a small group and wash hands before they begin to work on their bananas.

- Show the bananas in a bunch, noting that this is the way they grow on trees.

- Pass out bananas cut into thirds, and assist the children in peeling them if necessary.

- Pass out plastic knives, assisting their grip if toddlers want help (many will want to do it themselves).

- Discuss what happens; describe the sawing motion, the pushing down, and how the banana feels compared to the peel.

Limits

- All materials remain on the table. Provide alternatives for play when toddlers lose interest or are finished.

- Encourage toddlers to cut up the bananas before eating them. Scheduling this experience *after* a snack rather than before may help toddlers focus on the cutting rather than the eating.

Other Things to Think About

- Scoring one strip of the peel helps toddlers peel the banana themselves.
- Combine with other simple cooking projects, such as pudding (see page 137).

Supporting Play

Use these strategies, shown in the following scenario, to foster toddlers' coordination practice:

- Provide opportunities for practice at varied levels of skill.
- Make room for trial and error and repeated investigation.
- Facilitate problem solving.

"We have a piece of banana for each of you," caregiver Suzanne says as four toddlers seat themselves at a table. "First, we have to peel it." Holding up a bunch of bananas, she says, "This is the way bananas grow on trees—together in bunches hanging down. Then they are picked and shipped to the store, and we buy them and eat them." Twenty-seven-month-old Jennifer says, "Like it," as she peels away a strip of banana peel. Twenty-nine-month-old Diane points out, "Me already did." She tears down each strip. Eighteen-month-old Juan allows the caregiver to get the peel started, but then grabs it back, shaking his head. Two-year-old Jo-Jo plays with his banana skin like a puppet, draping it over his hand. After everyone laughs, Suzanne hands out plastic knives, saying, "We can cut up these bananas for eating. Knives are for cutting, and bananas are for eating. Here, Juan, try to hold the knife by the handle." Juan is shaking his head, "No show, no."

Pretend Boots

The thick plastic bags that disposable diapers are packaged in may be recycled into pretend boots for play in a wet yard. Toddlers can experience the joy of puddle stomping while caregivers and parents appreciate dry shoes. This is particularly fun if it's been too wet to be outdoors for a while.

What You'll Need

- Enough plastic bags (thick, as from disposable diaper packaging) to offer boots for all in the group.
- Masking tape.
- A wet yard.

What to Do

- When the rain stops and the yard is wet, it is the perfect time to offer these pretend boots.
- Caregivers can cover their shoes first, modeling pretend boots.
- Toddlers shoes can be covered by placing their feet in the plastic bags and securing comfortably with masking tape around the ankle or lower leg.

Limits

- If the child does not want the boots initially, offer a choice: "Do you want to stay inside or go out with the boots on?"

Other Things to Think About

- Toddlers who have their own boots but have been reluctant to wear them may want to wear their own rather than these pretend ones.

Supporting Play

The caregiver took advantage of a spontaneous idea to model the following strategies in the scenario below.

- Allow for innovative use of materials.

- Facilitate problem solving with observation and open-ended questions.

"What donin?" thirty-one-month-old Margo asks caregiver Annie. "I'm putting on my pretend boots so we can go out into the yard. The sand is still wet and there are some puddles." "Rain?" Margo asks. "No, the rain has stopped. Margo, do you want some boots?" Annie asks. "Yes!" says Margo. She sits down in front of Annie to get the boots on over her shoes. Twenty-six-month-old Roger doesn't want any boots on his feet and chooses to stay inside. Thirty-month-old Lanie says "I have real boots!" "You have real red boots," Annie responds. Soon four toddlers are ready to go outdoors with Annie. Parker runs through a puddle, turning around to jump into it with both feet. Glee is evident all over his face. "It's good to be outdoors again, isn't it?" Annie comments. Eighteen-month-old Avi slides his booted feet, almost like skating. The plastic makes noise on the cement. Margo and Lanie head for the sand. They look behind them to see their footprints.

Tube Hummer with Holes

Older toddlers can coordinate their breath and fingers to play this simple and fun instrument. They can decorate the instruments themselves and, with the caregiver's help, punch holes to complete the instrument.

What You'll Need

- Cardboard tubes (like toilet-tissue tubes).
- Markers, stickers, or paint to decorate tubes.
- Handheld hole puncher.
- Waxed paper, precut into rounds or squares to fit over one end of a tube.
- Tape to fasten waxed paper over one tube end.

What to Do

- Have materials ready.
- Gather a small group of toddlers, explaining that "Today you will make your own musical instrument."
- Have toddlers begin to decorate their tubes. If children ask for other decorative materials, provide them if at all possible.
- As each child is ready, hold your hand over theirs so they can feel the pressure as you punch two to three holes along the length of each tube.
- As toddlers finish their decorating, help them place the waxed paper over one end, securing it with tape.
- Play the instrument by blowing through the open end. Reflect discoveries about the feel of vibrations and the varying sounds produced.

Limits

- Punching the holes will be fascinating to toddlers. Use phrases like these to help children wait for a turn:

Everyone will get a turn.

Thanks for waiting.

You can add more decorations while you wait.

Watch closely so you'll be ready.

Do you want to put stickers on first or punch the holes first?

- Part of the point of the decorating process is to easily identify one's own instrument.

- For sanitary reasons, each toddler should play only his own instrument.

Other Things to Think About

- This experience might be followed up by playing real recorders, flutes, or other wind instruments.

- This experience might be combined with other instruments for an impromptu parade.

Supporting Play

Use these strategies, shown in the following scenario, to support children's play:

- Promote body awareness.

- Allow for trial and error and repeated investigation.

After decorating the cardboard tubes to make hummer instruments, the toddlers are ready to play them. Three holes are punched in each tube, and the waxed paper is attached, as the other toddlers work with decorations. Pan is very excited, as caregiver Edna invites the toddlers to sit on the floor for a concert. Pan, twenty-eight months old, begins to blow through the tube. "Try it through the open end," Edna suggests. Anne and Lynnette, both thirty months, blow into their tubes. Anne stops when she hears the sound. "That's you making music!" Edna tells her. Lynnette giggles, "It tickles." "Oh, you can feel the vibrations your humming makes. That's what makes the music—the tickling vibrations." Lizzie, thirty-five months old, is the first one to pay attention to the holes. She carefully places her fingers over them, and blows. "How does that sound now?" Edna asks.

Bottles and Jars with Lids

Toddlers love to match lids and open and close bottles and jars. Toddlers can use their senses to look, feel, and problem solve which lid goes with which bottle, testing their hypotheses. This experience is similar to doing puzzles. Toddlers can practice the coordinated movements of screwing and unscrewing lids over and over.

What You'll Need

- Assortment of plastic bottles, jars, and their lids (three or four for each toddler).
- Trays or baskets for sorting or carrying.

What to Do

- Set up the jars and lids in trays or baskets on a table in groups of three or four.
- Invite a small group of toddlers to investigate what is on the table.
- Facilitate taking turns and trading between the toddlers.

Limits

- Help toddlers anticipate when they are all done with this experience so they can go on to something else without exhibiting throwing or aggressive behavior. They can return if they wish and if the materials are available.

Other Things to Think About

- Provide small items for toddlers to place in the bottles or jars if they wish.
- Increase the types of containers as toddlers' coordination skills develop. Consider using plastic food-storage containers, covered mixing bowls, or boxes with close-fitting lids.

Supporting Play

Use these strategies, shown in the following scenario, to support children's coordination skills:

- Make room for trial and error and repeated investigation.

- Facilitate problem solving with observation and open-ended questions.

> *Thirty-month-old Penny says, "Open this." Caregiver Phoebe responds, "Try unscrewing it," and demonstrates with hand motions. "I not screw," says Penny, but then starts doing it and the lid comes off. "You did it!" says Phoebe. Two-year-old Lynn easily pulls off a margarine lid top. Penny approaches Phoebe with another container. "I want this open," she says. "Try using your thumb to lift the edge of the lid," Phoebe suggests. After thirty seconds, Penny abandons the attempt and starts stacking the closed containers. Twenty-one-month-old Kelly is playing with the open containers. Holding one in her left hand, she swirls her right hand as if filling the container. Using both hands, she shakes it up before putting it to her face. Twenty-seven-month-old Ricardo walks to pick up a lid and its matching container, a few feet away. He stands, working for three minutes to get the screw lid on. Twenty-nine-month-old Jake approaches Penny, who has gone to do markers on a separate table. She points, "No, that goes on this." Jake asks, "Like this?" Penny says, "No, put the lid on." "Like this?" Jake asks again. " No," answers Penny. "Like this," Jake asks again. Penny says, "Yes, yeah."*

Index

Note: Specific experiences are designated as (I) for infants; (I/T) for infants/toddlers; or (T) for toddlers.

A

activities vs. experiences, 35
adults
  day-to-day experiences with children,
    importance of, 1, 2
  emotional connections with children, 16
  predisposition to guide children's learning, 1
  programmed to nurture children's
    development, 16
articulating needs and wants (comprehensive
  strategy), 9–10

B

Baby Gym (I), 68
Baby Hide-and-Seek (I), 54
Baby's Games (Slier), 76
Balancing Practice (I/T), 106
Big Fabric Pieces (I/T), 88
body awareness, promoting by coaching
  Baby Gym (I), 68
  Balancing Practice (I/T), 106
  Challenge Crawl (I), 62
  Hammering (T), 158
  Heavy, Light (T), 122
  Playdough (I/T), 103
  Ramps for Wheeled Vehicles (T), 164
  Step Right Up! (I), 70
  Tube Hummer with Holes (T), 170
  Walking Boards (I/T), 110
Bottles and Jars with Lids (T), 172
Boxes (I/T), 112

C

caregivers
  acknowledging children's feelings, 9, 11
  anticipating what's next, 9, 11
  articulating children's needs and wants, 9–10
  coordination of materials, time, children,
    and selves, 17
  defined, 5
  frustrations of, related to children's
    frustrations, 13, 16, 26
  high turnover rate, effects, 1
  inadequate compensation, balancing
    factors, 2
  interactions with children, 19–20, 24–25, 30
  job focus, 7, 11
  job satisfaction and turnover rate, 2
  modeling behavior, 8–9
  observation and optimal stress, 8, 11
  observing, supporting, and facilitating what
    children want to do, 33
  offering real choices, 10, 11
  routines and transitions, 8
  routines as valuable experiences, 7–8
  setting limits, 10–11
  shortage of experienced caregivers, 1
  think like an infant/toddler, 30, 31–32
Cellophane Gluing and Viewing (I/T), 84
Center for the Childcare Workforce, 2
Challenge Crawl (I), 62
charts
  environments, appropriate vs. inappropriate
    planning, 17, 21
  Think Like an Infant/Toddler, 31–32
  three Cs, 14

child-initiated interactions, responding to
  Everything Has a Name! (I), 44
children
    acknowledgment of feelings, 9, 11
    anticipating what's next, 9, 11
    articulating needs and wants, 9–10
    biting as response to pain or frustration, 30
    conflict as learning opportunity, 24
    connection and social and emotional
      development, 14, 15
    coordination and physical development, 14,
      15–16
    curiosity and cognitive development, 14, 15
    day-to-day experiences, importance of, 1, 2
    emotional connections with adults, 16
    emotional development and environment, 23
    everyday behaviors and stages of development,
      13–16
    frustrations of and caregivers' frustrations, 13,
      16, 26
    group care settings and individual attention, 16
    individual schedules vs. group activities, 18, 23
    interactions with caregivers, 19–20, 24–25, 30
    interdependent relationships, 15
    learning how to learn, 35
    mastering small- and large-motor control, 20, 25
    modeling behavior, 8–9
    observation and optimal stress, 8, 11
    offering real choices to, 10, 11
    physical environment and frustrations, 13, 16
    play as learning, 16, 33
    practicing physical skills vs. limited physical
      activity, 20–21, 25–26
    predisposition to learn, 1
    problem behaviors, and alterations of
      environment, 2
    programs for, basis, 2
    routines as valuable experiences, 7
    setting limits for, 10–11
    sharing, not advocated, 10
    small group play vs. inhibited or hurtful
      interactions, 19, 23–24
    think like an infant/toddler, 30, 31–32
    See also Infants; Toddlers
children's needs, meeting predictably and
  consistently

Fingerplays (I), 74
  Mirroring (I/T), 98
  Shadow Puppets (T), 149
  Soft Puppets (T), 146
choices, offering (comprehensive
    strategy), 10, 11
Choo-Choo (T), 140
Clap Hands (fingerplays), 75
"Clean" Fingerpainting (I/T), 82
Cobbler, Cobbler Mend My Shoe (fingerplays), 76
cognitive development, curiosity and, 14
Colored Bubble Art (T), 156
Colored Cellophane on a Sunny Window (I), 40
communication, 14
communication, honoring verbal and nonverbal
  Everything Has a Name! (I), 44
  Mirroring (I/T), 98
comprehensive caring strategies, 7–11, 14
    acknowledging children's feelings, 9, 11
    anticipating transitions, unusual events, and
      changes in routines, 9, 11
    articulating needs and wants, 9–10
    modeling behavior, 8–9
    observation and optimal stress, 11
    offering real choices, 10, 11
    setting consistent limits, 10–11
connection
    emotional connections between children and
      adults, 16
    and social and emotional development, 14, 15
    three Cs (chart), 14
Con-Tact Paper Collage (I/T), 77
coordination
    of materials, time, caregivers, and children, 17
    and physical development, 14, 15–16
    three Cs (chart), 14
curiosity
    and cognitive development, 14, 15
    and single or limited-use toys, 17
    three Cs chart, 14
Cutting Bananas (T), 166

D

definitions, 5

E

emotional development
    connection and, 15
    and environment, 23
environment
    altering, to deal with problem behaviors, 2
    changes, deciding what to change, 27
    children's frustration with, 13, 16, 26
    defined, 16
    evaluation of, 26–27
    flexible vs. inflexible environments, 18, 23
    group size, considerations, 28–29
    individual schedules vs. group activities,
        18, 23
    interactions among caregivers and children,
        19–20, 24–25, 30
    materials
        choice of, presentation and arrangement,
            27–30
        open-ended, multiple-use vs. single,
            limited-use, 17–18, 22–23
        relating to children's interests vs. caregivers'
            interests, 17, 22
    observation of, and modification, 30, 32–33
    outdoor environments and infants, 29
    planning
        appropriate planning (chart), 21
        generally, 13–33
        lacking a developmental foundation, effects,
            16–21
        licensing, health, and safety regulations, 26
        meeting developmental needs, 26–33
        nonexistent or inappropriate planning
        (chart), 17
        sensitive to development, 21–26
    pockets of play, 28–29
    practicing physical skills vs. limited physical
        activity, 20–21, 25–26
    small group play vs. inhibited or hurtful
        interactions, 19, 23–24
    small play areas vs. undifferentiated areas or
        separate rooms, 18, 19, 21, 23–24
    think like an infant/toddler, 30, 31–32
Everything Has a Name! (I), 44
experiences vs. activities, 35

extend exploration using child's interest as guide
    Baby Hide-and-Seek (I), 54
    Cellophane Gluing and Viewing (I/T), 84
    Gluing Collage on Foil (T), 124
    Make Your Own Playdough! (T), 129
    Making Music, Hearing Sounds (I), 56
    Water Pillow (I), 66
Eyer, Dianne Widmeyer
    Infants, Toddlers, and Caregivers, 5–6
    Ten Principles of Respectful Caregiving, 5–6

F

Family Boxes (I), 58
family culture
    Family Boxes (I), 58
    Introduce Cultural Variations of Home Life
        (I/T), 100
    Making Pudding (T), 137
feelings, acknowledging (comprehensive
    strategy), 9, 11
Find-and-Pull Toys (I), 64
Fingerplays (I), 74
for every no, give two yeses, 11
    Hanging Sounds (I/T), 96
Frozen Fruits and Vegetables (I), 46
Fun with Flashlights (T), 132

G

Gluing Collage on Foil (T), 124
Gonzales-Mena, Janet
    for every no give two yeses, 11
    Infants, Toddlers, and Caregivers, 5–6
    optimal stress, 8
    Ten Principles of Respectful Caregiving, 5–6
Gopnik, Alison
    babies are born knowing how to organize
        information from their senses, 16
    the company of adults is school for babies, 2
    The Scientist in the Crib: Minds, Brains, and How
        Children Learn, 1, 15
    toys as "lab equipment" for experiments, 19

H

Hammering (T), 158
Hanging Balls Outdoors (T), 161
Hanging Sounds (I/T), 96
Heavy, Light (T), 122

I

infants
    defined, 5
    and outdoor environments, 29
    planned experiences, 40–121
    think like an infant, 30, 31–32
    See also Children
Infants, Toddlers, and Caregivers (Gonzales-Mena
        and Eyer), 6
Infant Shape Sorter (I), 72
Introduce Cultural Variations of Home Life (I/T),
        100
introduce peers and adults by name
    Photo Albums and Pages (I/T), 90

K

Kuhl, Patricia K., *The Scientist in the Crib: Minds,
        Brains, and How Children Learn*, 1, 15

L

limits, consistent setting of (comprehensive
        strategy), 10–11

M

Make Your Own Playdough! (T), 129
Making Music, Hearing Sounds (I), 56
Making Pudding (T), 137
Markers (I/T), 108
materials
    choice of, presentation and arrangement, 27–30
    open-ended, multiple-use vs. single, limited-
        use, 17–18, 22–23
    relating to children's interests vs. caregivers'
        interests, 17, 22

materials, choice of and time to manipulate
    Baby Gym (I), 68
    "Clean" Fingerpainting (I/T), 82
    Observation and Experimentation with Water
        (T), 126
    Sprouting Seeds (T), 134
    Texture Mat (I), 52
    Water Balls (I/T), 120
materials, innovative use
    Colored Bubble Art (T), 156
    Con-Tact Paper Collage (I/T), 77
    Hanging Balls Outdoors (T), 161
    Papier-Mâché (T), 152
    Pretend Boots (T), 168
    Tube Rollers (I/T), 117
Meltzoff, Andrew N., *The Scientist in the Crib:
        Minds, Brains, and How Children Learn*, 1, 15
Mirroring (I/T), 98
Mirrors (I), 48
modeling behavior (comprehensive strategy), 8–9
mutual interests, affirming to encourage
        interdependence, 142
    Choo-Choo (T), 140
    Family Boxes (I), 58
    Hanging Sounds (I/T), 96
    Introduce Cultural Variations of Home Life
        (I/T), 100
    Making Pudding (T), 137
    Photo Albums and Pages (I/T), 90
    Real Keys on Key Rings (T), 144
    Shadow Puppets (T), 149
    Velcro Lids (I/T), 93
My Turtle (fingerplays), 75

O

observation
    and optimal stress (caring strategy), 8, 11
    and planning an environment, 22, 26, 30, 32–33
Observation and Experimentation with Water (T),
        126
offer information ("Say what you know")
    Big Fabric Pieces (I/T), 88
    Cellophane Gluing and Viewing (I/T), 84
    Fun with Flashlights (T), 132
    Gluing Collage on Foil (T), 124

offer information, cont.
  Make Your Own Playdough! (T), 129
  Observation and Experimentation with Water
    (T), 126
  Sensory Immersion (I), 50
  Texture Mat (I), 52
One Thing At a Time (I), 60
optimal stress (caring strategy), 8, 11

P

Palo Alto Infant-Toddler Center, 3
Papier-Mâché (T), 152
Parachute and Ball Play (T), 142
Peekaboo Scarf (I), 42
Photo Albums and Pages (I/T), 90
physical development, coordination and, 15–16
planned experiences
  choosing, 36–37
  generally, 35–36
  infants, 40–121
  toddlers, 77–173
  using, 37
planning an environment
  appropriate planning (chart), 21
  generally, 13–33
  lacking a developmental foundation, effects,
    16–21
  licensing, health, and safety regulations, 26
  meeting developmental needs, 26–33
  nonexistent or inappropriate planning (chart), 17
  sensitive to development, 21–26
play, what children's learning looks like to adults, 16
Playdough (I/T), 103
Playdough (T), 129
Pretend Boots (T), 168
problem solving, facilitating with observation
    and open-ended questions
  Bottles and Jars with Lids (T), 172
  Boxes (I/T), 112
  Challenge Crawl (I), 62
  Cutting Bananas (T), 166
  Infant Shape Sorter (I), 72
  Papier-Mâché (T), 152
  Playdough (I/T), 103
  Pretend Boots (T), 168

problem solving, cont.
  Ramps for Wheeled Vehicles (T), 164
  Water Balls (I/T), 120

R

Ramps for Wheeled Vehicles (T), 164
Real Keys on Key Rings (T), 144
recipes
  Playdough, 103
  Uncooked Playdough, 129
respectful caregiving, principles of, 5–6
routines, anticipating changes in (comprehensive
    strategy), 9

S

scenarios
  caterpillar-to-butterfly lesson (Wanda), 18, 21,
    22–23, 35
  eating schedules and single-function rooms
    (Blaine, Eloise, Ned), 19, 21, 24
  infants and physical activity (Muna), 20, 21, 25
  outdoor pockets of play, 29
  picnic birthday party (Vanessa), 36–37
  Ten Principles of Respectful Caregiving, 6–7, 11
  toddlers and toys in undivided room (Jan),
    19–20, 21, 24–25
*The Scientist in the Crib: Minds, Brains, and How
    Children Learn* (Gopnik, Meltzoff, and Kuhl),
    1, 15
self-awareness, promoting
  Baby Hide-and-Seek (I), 54
  Frozen Fruits and Vegetables (I), 46
  Mirrors (I), 48
  Weight Fleece (I/T), 86
Sensory Immersion (I), 50
Seven Comprehensive Strategies, 7–11, 14
Shadow Puppets (T), 149
share personal interests ("Say who you are")
  Big Fabric Pieces (I/T), 88
  Colored Cellophane on a Sunny Window (I), 40
  Sprouting Seeds (T), 134
  Weight Fleece (I/T), 86
  What Are You Wearing Today? (I/T), 80
sharing among children, not advocated, 10

skills, opportunities to practice at varied levels
    Baby Gym (I), 68
    Cutting Bananas (T), 166
    Hammering (T), 158
    Hanging Balls Outdoors (T), 161
    Heavy, Light (T), 122
    Markers (I/T), 108
    Playdough (I/T), 103
    Step Right Up! (I), 70
    Tube Rollers (I/T), 117
    Velcro Balls and Paddles (I/T), 114
    Walking Boards (I/T), 110
Slier, Debby
    Baby's Games, 76
slow the pace; be available ("Be an island")
    Choo-Choo (T), 140
    Fingerplays (I), 74
    Mirroring (I/T), 98
    One Thing At a Time (I), 60
    Soft Puppets (T), 146
social development, connection and, 15
Soft Puppets (T), 146
Sprouting Seeds (T), 134
Step Right Up! (I), 70

T

taking turns and trading
    Real Keys on Key Rings (T), 144
    Soft Puppets (T), 146
    Velcro Lids (I/T), 93
Ten Principles of Respectful Caregiving, 5–6
Texture Mat (I), 52
Think Like an Infant/Toddler (chart), 31–32
This Little Cow East Grass (fingerplays), 76
three Cs (chart), 14
    See also Connection; Coordination; Curiosity
toddlers
    defined, 5
    planned experiences, 77–173
    think like a toddler, 30, 31–32
    See also Children
toys
    arranging to suggest exploration, 28
    "lab equipment" for experiments, 19
    and limited play possibilities, 17

transitions, anticipating (comprehensive strategy), 9, 11
trial-and-error and repeated investigation
    Bottles and Jars with Lids (T), 172
    Boxes (I/T), 112
    Colored Bubble Art (T), 156
    Con-Tact Paper Collage (I/T), 77
    Cutting Bananas (T), 166
    Find-and-Pull Toys (I), 64
    Infant Shape Sorter (I), 72
    Ramps for Wheeled Vehicles (T), 164
    Tube Hummer with Holes (T), 170
    Velcro Balls and Paddles (I/T), 114
Tube Hummer with Holes (T), 170
Tube Rollers (I/T), 117

U

unusual events, anticipating (comprehensive strategy), 9

V

validate child's experience ("Say what you see")
    Cellophane Gluing and Viewing (I/T), 84
    "Clean" Fingerpainting (I/T), 82
    Colored Cellophane on a Sunny Window (I), 40
    Frozen Fruits and Vegetables (I), 46
    Fun with Flashlights (T), 132
    Mirrors (I), 48
    Observation and Experimentation with Water (T), 126
    Peekaboo Scarf (I), 42
    Sensory Immersion (I), 50
Velcro Balls and Paddles (I/T), 114
Velcro Lids (I/T), 93

W

Walking Boards (I/T), 110
Water Balls (I/T), 120
Water Pillow (I), 66
Weight Fleece (I/T), 86
What Are You Wearing Today? (I/T), 80